"This is a really enjoyable book. [...] people and passion for the Bible [...] least understood promises in all of scripture. Highly practical but full of inspiration and encouragement, *Imagine* will warm your heart, deepen your faith and strengthen your steps as you walk forward into all that God has for your life."

Chris Cartwright, General Superintendent. Elim churches

"Faith is always an adventure, and adventures are sometimes scary but never boring. Simon Lawton's first book helps us think through what it might mean to hear the voice of God and follow wherever He might lead us, even when it is through the unpredictable space of an open door.

"Read this book intentionally. Let it soak through your soul and revitalise long-forgotten dreams. Let it reignite your hunger for God and yearning to see Him move again. Here you will find inspiration for the discouraged, hope for the despairing and grace for the fearful. Let the God of whom Simon speaks touch you through his words and bring life to your soul again."

Malcolm Duncan, pastor, author, theologian, broadcaster, FRSA

"Just as a car needs an MOT, our souls also need a regular tune-up. This timely 'manual' will jump-start your faith and get your trust spark plugs firing properly again. While this is a helpful and practical book, it is not just about maintenance. Simon dares us to imagine a life where we truly trust God for the entire journey ahead. Buckle up, get into gear and start reading. I guarantee you'll be glad you did."

Cathy Madavan, writer, speaker and author of Digging for Diamonds.

"Where there is no vision the people perish (Proverbs 29:18). Pastor Simon's *Imagine* is a joy to drink in. You'll hear the heart of a pastor about the good Shepherd and how victory comes in bite-sized pieces. Partake in Pastor Simon's feast. He serves it up to us in every page of this book!"

Michele Pillar, three times Grammy-nominated singer, speaker and author of Untangled: The Truth Will Set You Free

"Simon's honest and often humorous approach is refreshing. His combination of personal stories with the use of relevant scripture emphasises the importance of getting God's perspective on everything! Although we each have a unique path, I'm sure at some point you will be able to identify with some of the trust issues Simon describes including some of the scenarios. A number of times I found myself saying: 'That was me too!'

"Whatever season of life you are currently in, this book aims to bring you encouragement and hope. Simon challenges us to imagine the impact it would have if we really did trust the Lord with all our hearts. By reading this book, I hope your own levels of faith will ignite, and you will be able to imagine new possibilities. Simon's life testifies to this, and to the incredible lengths and intricate details God goes to on our behalf."

Lara Martin, music minister

IMAGINE

TRUSTING GOD
LIKE NEVER BEFORE

simon lawton

ISBN 978 1 99964 890 9
e-ISBN 978 1 99964 891 6

First edition 2018

Contents

Acknowledgements

I would like to say a special thank you to a couple of people who have helped me produce this book. To Joy Tibbs for her constant encouragement and insightful work as editor, and to Leila Egerton for her fantastic cover design.

I'd also like to thank all the pastors and leaders who have invested in and mentored me over the years, particularly Rev Michael Haighton and Rev Stuart Clarke, who saw something in me that no one else did. I wouldn't be in ministry today if it wasn't for those guys.

I couldn't have written *Imagine* without the encouragement and support of the two amazing congregations I have pastored in Crewe and Newcastle as I learned to trust Jesus more myself.

Thank you to my parents, Janet and Philip Lawton, for choosing to adopt me into your family at just a few weeks old. You instilled faith and trust in God in me from an early age, and I have never looked back. I will be forever grateful.

A massive thank you to my wonderful and growing family. My amazing wife Julia has been an incredible support during this crazy, challenging journey of life and ministry. The call to ministry, and to becoming a minister's wife, is not for the fainthearted. She carries it well. Love you, Jules. x

And finally (just like in my sermons!), thanks be to my amazing Father in heaven, who revealed Himself to me at an early age and has proven Himself completely worthy of my trust. He is also worthy of yours.

Introduction

Trusting God as we never had before

It was a cool, damp autumn morning in September 1992 when we closed the front door of our beautiful family home in Leicester for the final time. We were leaving behind countless amazing memories of family gatherings, children's parties and the birthplace of our first daughter, Sarah. We loved that house, and we haven't lived in such a wonderful home since.

We were heading for Bible college close to the quiet little market town of Nantwich in Cheshire. We crammed the last of our belongings into the tiny Metro – which was never intended to carry four young children and a TV on the back seat – and headed off into exciting future we believed God had for us.

Our friends thought we had lost the plot, and some family members warned us against the move. Looking at it logically, we had failed to sell our house, had no tenants to cover the mortgage payments, no income, no student grant, no money to pay the rent for our tiny two-bedroomed house in Nantwich (yes, two beds for a family of six!), no money for college fees, and tax debts of some £13,000. To cap it all, we had a couple of days' worth of food and I had just five pounds in my wallet. Looking back, it may have appeared naive or just plain crazy. However, one thing we did have was an incredible trust in the God who had called us to this huge ministry adventure.

A friend and I had moved the family furniture and belongings a couple of nights earlier in a loaned horse box – a smelly contraption full of straw and other horsey items – as we couldn't afford a removals company. On arrival, our two eldest sons were allocated the front room of the terraced house as their bedroom, which became the dining room at mealtimes, and they were woken by the postman at some ungodly hour every morning.

Over the coming weeks and months, God proved Himself worthy of our trust. He had already provided places for our three boys at one of the best local schools, and a lady we had never met before miraculously knocked on the door with fresh vegetables and groceries the following day. The house was provided at zero rent for the first few months, and within a few weeks we found tenants for our old home. A government maintenance grant followed, and a family member offered to pay a term's worth of my college fees each academic year. Amazingly, all our debts were cleared while I was studying. God is worthy of our trust, but in order to discover this He allows us to be taken to the brink at times, and will often ask us to step into the unknown.

During this period, we learned to trust God in ways we never had before. He has proven Himself completely trustworthy. We have been in ministry now for twenty-plus years, and have seen God's faithfulness over and over again. He is amazing. I've often tried to imagine what our lives would have been like had we not trusted God and taken that journey to Bible college in 1992. However, as I look even further back, I realise that trusting God had already become a central tenet of my faith, and that the call to Nantwich was just part of the journey of faith God had called me to travel down.

I'm convinced that we have each been uniquely shaped by God to live out exciting lives that have been specifically planned by our creator just for us. I'm especially convinced, as I look back, that there is a place or a niche where we each fit; a place where we can feel fulfilled, while at the same time fulfilling God's purposes on earth. That is an incredible place to be, and I believe that, for the most part over the past fifty-plus years of my life, I have lived out that God-shaped purpose.

I hope this book will inspire you to trust Him. To *really* trust Him. Imagine what your life could be like if you totally trusted Him. I am totally convinced that if we trust God like we never have before, we will live like we never have before!

Solomon, the wisest man who ever lived, said this:

"Trust in the Lord with all your heart and lean not on your own understanding; in all your ways submit to him, and he will make your paths straight" (Proverbs 3:5-6).

Solomon learned this for himself, having witnessed his father David's deep trust and faith in God, and he shared his valuable wisdom with us. We would all do well to take on board Solomon's wisdom, but also to recognise that it comes from a God who has a different perspective from our worldly perspectives; whose ways are clearly not our ways; the One who isn't changed or influenced by passing fads and trends.

Imagine if you really did:

- Trust in the Lord with all your heart
- Stop leaning on your own understanding
- Acknowledge and submit to Him
- Walk along straight paths

Imagine the impact on your relationship with God, faith, family and other relationships; on your career, ambitions, dreams, finances and health. Imagine the doors God might open and the adventures, experiences and relationships you might enjoy. Imagine the lasting legacy you might leave behind for generations to come.

With more than twenty years' experience as a pastor, I believe that trusting God is one of the biggest issues for many Christians. Tragically, I meet many who simply refuse to trust God with every aspect of their lives. They can't bring themselves to totally surrender and submit their lives to Jesus Christ. That's a tragedy, as they are missing out on much that God has for them.

Can I challenge you?
Come on a journey of exploration with me. It doesn't matter what age you are. Maybe you're just starting out on your life journey, or maybe you're middle-aged or in the latter years of your life. However young or old you are, it's never too late to really start trusting God again with your life and your future. No one can predict the incredible adventures, experiences and new relationships He has in store for you.

There shouldn't be any 'no-go' areas in our lives, but sadly there are for each one of us. As you read this book, I want to encourage you to start your journey with a simple commitment to trust Jesus again and determine to make Him Lord of all. It begins with a simple commitment and continues as a journey of faith. God will allow you to be tested along the way, but let me tell you that you are in for a far more exciting life than you ever thought possible.

Part I

Purposeful trust

"Life would be so wonderful if we only knew what to do with it"
(Greta Garbo).[i]

Chapter 1

God has a plan for your life

When I was a little boy, all I wanted to be was a train driver. As I got older, I wanted to become a professional footballer, scoring goals for my beloved Leicester City and England. In my teens, I decided I wanted to be a vet until I realised biology wasn't one of my strongest subjects.

By the time I had left school, I wanted to be a retail manager, and was making good progress in my career until God stepped in and called me into pastoral ministry. During my life, I've run my own business, led many different ministries in churches, successfully planted a church, headed up two Christian summer camps and served as a football chaplain. This is all on top of being a husband, a father to five adult children, and a grandfather to an ever-expanding number of grandchildren.

For the most part, my life has been a wonderful experience. In spite of the difficulties, challenges, attacks, disappointments, bereavements, failures and losses, I can honestly say that it has been God's plan for me. I sincerely hope that I haven't missed out on anything He had uniquely shaped me for or planned for me to do.

"For we are God's handiwork, created in Christ Jesus to do good works, which God prepared in advance for us to do" (Ephesians 2:10).

My hope in writing this book is to encourage everyone who reads it to grasp the fact that God has a unique plan and purpose for each of us, and to trust Him enough to allow His purposes and plans to be outworked in our lives. That's incredibly exciting!

The search for meaning and purpose
It is my belief that most people are searching for personal identity, meaning and fulfilment. You only have to walk around an airport bookshop to see this. These stores are full of self-help books that aim to make us happy, maximise our lives and realise our dreams.

Countless millions meander through their lives in the full knowledge that something is missing. It's almost as if there is a massive cavity in their hearts that they simply cannot fill themselves. They do their level best to fill this gaping hole with all kinds of things that might provide temporary satisfaction, but they remain completely unsatisfied. Relationship with God has to be the starting point, and once we get to know Him He will begin to fill the hole. As His plans and purposes begin to increase in our lives, the hole will become smaller and smaller.

Ask yourself: "What am I actually looking to get out of life?"
This is one of the critical questions we should be asking. I'll hazard a guess that your response might include some or all of the following: great relationships, good health, leisure, pleasure, marriage, children, career, home and financial security. But surely there's more to life than this?

"Lord, remind me how brief my time on earth will be. Remind me that my days are numbered— how fleeting my life is. You have made my life no longer than the width of my hand. My entire lifetime is just a moment to you; at best, each of us is but a breath" (Psalms 39:4-5, NLT).

A person who lives for seventy years will experience more than twenty-five thousand days, but what are we supposed to do with the brief time we have on earth?

"Our greatest fear should not be of failure but of succeeding at things in life that don't really matter"[vii] (Tim Kizziar).

What is God's plan for my life?
I'm amazed at how many people race through their twenty-five thousand or so days without even considering whether God has a plan for their lives. The Bible suggests a creator who planned everything well, and who has a plan for our lives.

For you created my inmost being; you knit me together in my mother's womb. I praise you because I am fearfully and wonderfully made; your works are wonderful, I know that full well. My frame was not hidden from you when I was made in the secret place, when I was woven together in the depths of the earth. Your eyes saw my unformed body; all the days ordained for me were written in your book before one of them came to be. (Psalm 139:13-16).

This suggests that God saw me even as my body was being formed in my mother's womb, and that He already had a plan for my life.

The Message version puts these verses like this:

Oh yes, you shaped me first inside, then out; you formed me in my mother's womb. I thank you, High God—you're breathtaking! Body and soul, I am marvellously made! I worship in adoration—what a creation! You know me inside and out, you know every bone in my body; You know exactly how I was made, bit by bit, how I was sculpted from nothing into something. Like an open book, you watched me grow from conception to birth; all the stages of my life were spread out before you, The days of my life all prepared before I'd even lived one day.

God has a plan for our lives, and it's a good one. In fact, as Judah Smith states:

"I believe that the only way to make sense out of this life is to include God in our plans and equations."[iii]

"For I know the plans I have for you," declares the Lord, "plans to prosper you and not to harm you, plans to give you hope and a future" (Jeremiah 29:11).

The trick is to plug into the unique plan God has prepared for each of us as individuals. I believe this is absolutely critical to living life to the absolute full (see John 10:10).

God's plan involves you (yes, you!)

God's plan for us as individuals is part of His overall plan for everyone; His plan of redemption and restoration for the whole of mankind.

"It's in Christ that we find out who we are and what we are living for. Long before we first heard of Christ and got our hopes up, he had his eye on us, had designs on us for glorious living, part of the overall purpose he is working out in everything and everyone" (Ephesians 1:11-12, MSG).

For some of us, it's hard to grasp that anyone, never mind the God of the universe, would involve us in His plans, yet His Word clearly states that He has, and does.

When I was a child, we would pick teams for each football game. The two captains would naturally pick the best players first, then the good players. There would be one or two left who nobody really wanted on their team because they weren't much good. Thankfully, I was OK as a player (I had a good engine, which made up for any lack of ability), but it was awful for those the captains didn't want to select. They must have felt unloved and unwanted.

Some of us go through our lives believing we are unloved and unwanted, but that is the opposite of how God sees us. When we consider how others view us, we find it hard to believe that God would see us any differently. Several years ago, while preparing a message for a group of young people, I received a wonderfully releasing revelation for the people there that night. It was a simple yet profound statement:

"God thought you were worth creating."

I have shared it numerous times over the years, and seen God set people free from the lies and misconceptions the enemy has sown into their lives. I have watched as they were released to be themselves. Sadly, so many people today have identity issues and suffer with low self-esteem and poor body image.

The fact is, God went to a lot of trouble to put you on the planet. You were not a mistake. God intentionally placed you here. He formed you in your mother's womb, and you are fearfully and wonderfully made; intricately woven together to become the person you are today.

Paul describes us as *"God's handiwork'"* in Ephesians 2:10. There is no one else like you. No one has the unique mix of spiritual gifts, personality, passions, heart, abilities and experiences that combine to make you who you are. God created you that way, and He loves you. He thinks you're great. Isn't it time you simply enjoyed being you? I've often said over the years that there is true freedom in being the people God created us to be, and in enjoying being those people!

God's plan for your life is dependent on you being you

I remember feeling overwhelmed by all the amazingly godly men and women around me during my first year at Bible college. I didn't feel like my face fitted or that I had anything much to offer, but then one day in the morning devotions one of our lecturers preached on this verse, which set me free:

"But by the grace of God I am what I am, and his grace to me was not without effect. No, I worked harder than all of them – yet not I, but the grace of God that was with me" (1 Corinthians 15:10).

I realised in a moment that God loved me as I was. He simply wanted me to be myself; the best 'me' I could be. In fact, the apostle Paul had been a really bad person, persecuting the Church, and having godly people thrown in prison and murdered. He was present at and approving of Stephen's stoning. I realised that if Paul, with God's help, could get over that and be everything God had called him to be, so could I.

I made a very clear decision that day that I wasn't going to be intimidated a second longer by the great theologians and spiritual giants around me (many of whom I count are among my closest friends today) and that I was going to enjoy being myself. Paul says: *"I am, what I am!"* He refused to compete or compare himself with anyone, but he did allow God's grace to change and transform him.

I realised that God wanted me to accept myself the way He had created me to be with all my unique characteristics, strengths and weaknesses, gifts and abilities. This is what I wrote in my journal that day in October 1993:

"I cannot be anyone else – it's no use watching others or trying to be what others are in that sense. I have decided to be MYSELF and by God's grace to be and become what He has called me to be."

I would encourage you today to come to the same conclusion. Commit to being the person God created you to be and enjoy being yourself.

God's plan is better than ours
When I was a child, my parents would often announce on a Saturday morning that we were going on a trip to some stately home, and our response would be to groan. We already had our own plans for the day, which for me normally involved my mates and a football. In response to our complaints, my mother would usually say: "You know you'll enjoy it when you get there." I have to say that this was rarely true. However, I have discovered that God's plans have always proven to be much better than mine. Thank God that He overrules our plans on occasion.

"We can make our plans, but the Lord determines our steps" (Proverbs 16:9, NLT).

I used to think I knew it all when I was young (and some of my congregation probably think this is still the case!). In fact, I remember that as a young person one of my favourite expressions was, "That's obvious." How proud and sure of myself I was. I felt I knew what was best for my life rather than realising that it was actually the God who had created me who knew it all. More importantly (from my perspective), he knew what He had planned for young Simon, and what was best for his life.

I thank God that, as I have matured as a believer, I've realised God's way isn't simply the best way; it's the *only* way to enjoy life in all its fullness. I'm content these days to trust Him, follow Him and allow Him to be the one to direct my steps.

Getting God's perspective

It's worth remembering that we're just passing through this life, and it is fleeting. The Bible describes us as *"aliens"* and *"strangers"* in this land (see 1 Peter 2:11, NASB); pilgrims on a journey, preparing for eternity. It's helpful to keep this in mind. We're here for His glory, not our own.

"But [we are different, because] our citizenship is in heaven. And from there we eagerly await [the coming of] the Saviour, the Lord Jesus Christ" (Philippians 3:20, AMP).

We mustn't forget that this life is temporary, and that God wants us to trust and follow Him from the moment we receive Him as Lord and Saviour until we take that final breath.

Nothing has changed since Jesus called the first disciples and, in fact, earlier, when God called the likes of Abraham, Isaac, Jacob, Moses, Joshua, Esther, Samuel, David, Jeremiah and Isaiah. He still wants us to trust Him and fix our eyes on spending eternity with Him.

Making good use of the time we've been allocated

I hate queuing, and I can't stand wasting time. Whenever I go for a hospital appointment I take a book to read, and when I'm at the gym or in the car I listen to podcasts. Who said men can't do two things at once? I'm determined to make good use of the time I have each day.

It seems clear to me that God has given each of us limited time on earth, and surely it's our calling and duty to maximise those days. The psalmist says that: *"...all the days ordained for me were written in your book before one of them came to be"* (see Psalm 139:13-16).

This reminds me that God has a great plan and purpose for my life, and that I should learn to trust Him with that life because He had it all mapped out before I was born. It's an amazing plan full of people, places and experiences, some of which will be great, while others will challenge and develop me as a person for what lies ahead.

As we saw in Ephesians earlier, we have been created as God's handiwork to do good works. The particular works God has in mind for you are important, and they are different from the ones he has in mind for me or for anyone else.

Therefore, you must discover what God has specifically created you to do. Then you must do it to the best of your ability, with His help. God went to all the trouble of forming us in our mothers' wombs and uniquely shaping us for works he had prepared in advance, so we must make sure that we don't settle for visionless lives. God has more than that for every single one of us, and that includes you, my friend. We are His partners in the story of the world's redemption.

God's plan depends on us trusting Him
I recognise we're all on a unique spiritual journey today, and we're all at different stages along this road.

Some are:

- Searching and exploring the Christian faith
- New Christians
- Old-time Christians who have 'heard it all before'
- Feeling disillusioned with faith and ready to walk away
- Losing faith and trust in God because of the cards life has dealt you
- Struggling to imagine that life could be any better

We're all from different walks of life. Maybe you're unemployed, marginalised, divorced, studying, retiring, a single parent (I honour you), suffering from a chronic condition or a wealthy high-flyer. Maybe you feel like you've tried everything and nothing works. Regardless of our circumstances, God's plan from the very beginning was for us to trust and be in relationship with Him, and to rely on Him for everything. As I often say, if we trust God like we never have before, we will live like we never have before!

We're called to trust and follow Him. Everything we do in this world flows from that relationship of trust with our wonderful creator and Father. We simply have to reconnect and allow Him to become our spiritual satnav. Once we do, our lives, relationships, marriages, hopes and dreams, financial affairs, service and ministries – every single area of our lives – will be transformed. We will mature, develop, grow and become fruitful. In fact, I would suggest that we will become fulfilled in ways we never could have dreamed possible.

Living as you never have before

In my opinion, the key to really discovering the life God intended for you, and living as you never have before, can be found in Solomon's wisdom. We must learn to trust God completely. Solomon was the wisest man who ever lived, and we should also remember that his wisdom came from the God who has a completely different perspective from our worldly perspective, whose ways are clearly not our ways (see Isaiah 55:8). *The Message* version puts our famous key passage (Proverbs 3:5-6) brilliantly:

"Trust God from the bottom of your heart; don't try to figure out everything on your own. Listen for God's voice in everything you do, everywhere you go; he's the one who will keep you on track."

Don't miss out on the prize

I love summertime. I always look forward to the long days, warm weather and trips to the seaside, mountains and hills. God has created such an outstanding world for us to enjoy. However, there used to be one day in summer that I absolutely loathed. Sports day! Which genius decided that we needed athletics? And who decided that those of us who loved football needed our season curtailed for running, skipping, jumping and egg-and-spoon races? Suffice to say, I was pretty useless at athletics. It was never a good day, and I never brought home a prize.

"Do you not know that in a race all the runners run, but only one gets the prize? Run in such a way as to get the prize. Everyone who competes in the games goes into strict training. They do it to get a crown that will not last, but we do it to get a crown that will last forever. Therefore I do not run like someone running aimlessly; I do not fight like a boxer beating the air. No, I strike a blow to my body

*and make it my slave so that after I have preached to others, I
myself will not be disqualified for the prize* (1 Corinthians 9:24-27).

There is, of course, an eternal prize and an earthly prize. My desire is
not to miss either; by running intentionally, focusing on God, trusting
Him totally and disciplining myself to run in a way that will result in a
win.

I am so aware of the way God directed my paths from one
home (with my biological family) and placed me in a home where I
could know Him for myself. At just a few weeks old, he took hold of me
and sovereignly redirected my life. At that moment, I had no concept
of what lay ahead, but now, like the Apostle Paul, I am determined to
absolutely make sure that my life counts for God and makes a
difference in the lives of others. I am determined to *"...take hold of
that for which Christ Jesus took hold of me"* (Philippians 3:12).

Don't settle for second best in life

The world, our own flesh and the devil will tempt us to settle for
second best, yet God encourages us to live life with Him in all its
fullness. The world has such low expectations and expects us to live
within these boundaries, but God, our Father, wants us to live
buoyantly in faith and to deeply trust Him.

I believe one of the worst things we can do is settle for second
best when a life of trust and obedience will yield so much more.
Nothing is worth giving up or swapping for a life full of adventures,
faith challenges, new experiences and incredible times with God.
Occasionally, I meet Christians who have settled for a minimalistic,
mundane, safe and faithless 'faith'. My heart goes out to them. Why
have they settled for little more than safe religion? They're missing out
on the fullness of the Christian journey.

Faith needs to be lived out in trust and obedience day by day.
There is a risk involved in trusting and obeying God. Every time we say
no to Him we are saying yes to playing safe. Even worse, we are saying
yes to the enemy of our souls.

"There's no greater danger than playing it safe" (Nike).

When we spend our days resisting God (the Bible tells us to resist the other guy, by the way), we are settling for second best and missing out on all the blessings God had prepared for us. Who knows what lies around the corner for the man or woman who continually seeks to trust and obey Him?

"Then Jesus spoke to his disciples. He said, 'If anyone wants to follow me, he must say no to himself. He must pick up his cross and follow me. If he wants to save his life, he will lose it. But if he loses his life for me, he will find it'" (Matthew 16:24-25, NIRV).

I want to encourage you never to settle for a second-best Christian experience. There is so much more for you. I challenge you as you read this book to trust God more every day, in every situation, until it becomes second nature. Never forget that God is trustworthy!

"Your kingdom is an everlasting kingdom, and your dominion endures through all generations. The Lord is trustworthy in all he promises and faithful in all he does" (Psalm 145:13).

Imagine
I wonder how you imagined your life would turn out. What did you dream about as a child? Was your dream realised or were you like me: a million miles off the mark? Pause for a moment and re-evaluate your life. What are you looking to get from it? Have you grasped God's plan for your life? He has uniquely shaped you for His purposes, and His plans involve *you*. He thought you were worth creating. Make a choice right now to never settle for a second-best life, but rather to discover His plan for your life and to make good use of the time He has allocated you.

Maybe right now is a good moment to pause and recommit your life, your loved ones and your plans to Him. Ask Him to help you, as you read this book, to really trust Him. Give Him permission to speak to you in the areas where you struggle to trust Him, knowing that His best for you *really is* the best for you.

Chapter 2

Trust is the issue

In our early years of marriage, my wife Julia, who had been widowed only a couple of years previously, would get quite upset with me if I came home later than I had agreed. I might have worked a bit longer than planned, or bumped into a friend and been delayed. Having lost one husband, she found it really difficult not to worry, and to trust God that I would be OK whenever I was late. Trusting God with my life and many other things was a difficult issue for her during the early years of our marriage.

Julia's trust in God was almost completely eroded when her first husband died. After all, the worst thing that could have occurred actually happened to her. She had experienced one of the toughest experiences life could throw at her. It was little wonder that she was concerned by my late return from work or other activities. Trust is a massive issue today for so many of us.

We don't trust people

We don't trust people, and consequently we struggle to trust God. I have to admit that I struggle to trust others myself at times. There are lots of reasons why we don't trust people, and they often relate to bad experiences we've had. We live in a generation where trust levels are at an all-time low.

The impact of the fall is further-reaching than in our relationship with God. It has impacted our trust of other people. This, in turn, impacts our ability to trust God. It's a vicious circle, and we need to break the cycle by really trusting Him again.

A man's word used to be his bond, but this is no longer the case. Politicians lie, estate agents mislead us, holiday companies sell us holidays that don't represent the carefully taken pictures, supermarkets deceive us with offers and sales that aren't genuine, car salespeople try to sell us junk at high prices, and even our friends and family members let us down.

A recent Mori poll[iv] of 1,000 people that the most trusted people in the UK are:

1. Doctors 89%
2. Teachers 86%
3. Scientists 83%
4. Judges 82%
5. Newsreaders 69%
6. Clergymen/priests 66%
7. Police 65%
8. Man in the street 64%
9. Estate agents 24%
10. MPs 23%

I suspect that few of us are surprised by the findings, although I was more than a little disappointed that clergymen only hit sixty-six percent, being one myself!

Author of *The Speed of Trust: The One Thing That Changes Everything*, Stephen MR Covey, argues that trust is in decline everywhere. He cites a 2004 estimate, which claims that the act of complying with US federal rules and regulations *"put in place essentially due to a lack of trust"* at $1.1 trillion.[v] He also points readers to a study carried out by the Association of Certified Fraud Examiners, which estimates that the average American company loses six percent of its annual revenue to fraudulent activity. By contrast, a Watson Wyatt study showed that high-trust companies outperform low-trust companies by nearly three hundred percent.[vi]

In a recent *Reader's Digest* survey of most-trusted Americans[vii], President Obama came sixty-fifth, while actor Tom Hanks came first. This is a guy who gets paid for pretending to be someone else!

Trust has been eroded, and as a result we struggle to trust our Father God and to believe what He says in His Word.

Trusting God can be tough
With levels of trust already low, we are bombarded with negative news about politicians, salespeople, pastors and doctors, among

countless others. This only serves to undermine our ability to trust anyone, never mind God. Is it any wonder that ours is probably the least trusting generation that has ever lived? As a pastor, I have lost count of the number of times Christians have deceived me or have been found to have told lies of some kind. Our trust in people is constantly put to the test.

I believe that trusting God is one of the biggest challenges for us as Christians. Often we don't trust Him enough to submit to Him, obey His Word or do what He has specifically told us to do. In short, we don't trust Him at all.

The Barna Group recently carried out some research[viii] and drew this conclusion: *"Driven by social mores, few adults who believe they are Christian are willing to abandon worldly objectives in favour of seeking godliness. Only one out of five (22%) stated that they live in a way which makes them completely dependent upon God."* Follow-up research indicated that such dependence usually only emerges in times of crisis or suffering.

Sadly, many of us have been conditioned by the world around us to remain independent and not to rely on anyone, least of all God. We see others doing well ("thank you very much") without God, and believe we can achieve the same results without trusting Him. Wasn't this how Israel's downfall began?

Where it all began
Trust has been an issue since the fall of humanity. Prior to the fall, Adam and Eve experienced all of the following benefits.

Significance
God gave Adam a purpose for being that was to: *"rule over the fish in the sea and the birds in the sky, over the livestock and all the wild animals, and over all the creatures that move along the ground"* (Genesis 1:26). Adam did not have to search for significance because he already had it!

Security

Adam was totally safe and secure in God's presence. Everything he needed was provided: food, shelter, companionship; everything. He had no concept of a genuine need.

Acceptance

Adam had an intimate relationship with God. He could talk with him at any time and have His full attention. Then God created Eve so he had a sense of belonging; not just to God, but to another human being.

They were accepted by God and each other. They were naked and unashamed. They had nothing to hide or cover up. They had an intimate relationship with one another in God's presence. This is how God created us to be. His plan was for us to live our lives from a position of complete trust and security in Him. He wanted us to have a real sense of purpose, with no needs or worries, and to enjoy a deep sense of belonging.

The fall caused us to lose our sense of significance, security and acceptance in God. We stopped trusting Him completely for everything, became independent, and learned to 'survive' on our own. We were created to know, love and trust God, and for Him to be the centre of our universe. But if we're honest, this is an ongoing battle for most of us. John sums it up well:

Don't love the world's ways. Don't love the world's goods. Love of the world squeezes out love for the Father. Practically everything that goes on in the world—wanting your own way, wanting everything for yourself, wanting to appear important—has nothing to do with the Father. It just isolates you from him. The world and all its wanting, wanting, wanting is on the way out—but whoever does what God wants is set for eternity (1 John 2:15-17, MSG).

Re-establishing our lost trust

Once we come into relationship with God through Jesus, we can rediscover what was stolen from us at the fall. It's a wonderful and precious thing to trust in God; to discover the One who is unfailingly loving, consistent and true. Through faith in Christ, our lost trust can be regained and recovered.

However, we must be aware that our enemy, the devil, is still smarting at the fact that we have regained what he caused to be stolen. He will do his utmost to cause us to lose that trust again through his three main helpers: the world, the flesh and himself. We will deal with this in detail later, but I want to encourage you. No matter what your experience of this world or at the hands of others might be, begin to trust. Yes, really start to trust in God again.

The ongoing battle for trust

During the First World War, more than a million men fought and died during the Battle of the Somme as English and French soldiers engaged in trench warfare with the German army. From July to November 1916, they fought over a piece of land that was just thirty miles in length. Neither side gained much ground, but many priceless young lives were lost.

As Christians, we're still fighting a battle with the devil over a vital ground called 'trust' in our lives. Remember what happened with Adam?

"And the Lord God commanded the man, 'You are free to eat from any tree in the garden; but you must not eat from the tree of the knowledge of good and evil, for when you eat from it you will certainly die'" (Genesis 2:16-17).

As we know, the devil came along and almost immediately sowed the first seeds of distrust:

Now the serpent was more crafty than any of the wild animals the Lord God had made. He said to the woman, 'Did God really say, "You must not eat from any tree in the garden"?' The woman said to the serpent, 'We may eat fruit from the trees in the garden, but God did say, "You must not eat fruit from the tree that is in the middle of the garden, and you must not touch it, or you will die."' 'You will not certainly die,' the serpent said to the woman. 'For God knows that when you eat from it your eyes will be opened, and you will be like God, knowing good and evil.' (Genesis 3:1-5).

'Did God really say…?' was the challenge the devil gave, and he's continued to give it ever since. It's the devil's catchphrase. We must never forget that he is the "father of all lies" (see John 8:44). Among other things, he has subtly sought to undermine God's Word among His people, with both the promises it contains and the consequences of failing to obey it continually and successfully undermined. Sadly, many Christians fail to read the Word regularly. As a consequence, they suffer when the enemy challenges what God has said because they have nothing to answer back with.

"The grass withers and the flowers fade, but the word of our God stands forever" (Isaiah 40:8, NLT).

We really must learn to take God at His Word and trust what He says. We must learn to fight for that long-disputed ground of trust.

What stops us trusting God?
What is the main thing stopping you from trusting God right now? It appears to me that there are a number of reasons why we don't trust God. I've listed a few here.

God has let me down
I suspect there are many Christians who feel let down by God. You may be one of them. Maybe a loved one died despite your prayers for healing, a job was lost, a relationship ended prematurely, specific long-term prayers weren't answered in the way you would have liked or you're blaming God for how your life has developed. Perhaps you feel God should have intervened or protected you more in a situation.

Maybe you blame God for the many political, economic, sociological, financial and natural disasters in the world today. If God is sovereign, you may be wondering why He allows suffering, sickness and financial crashes.

Independent spirit
Maybe you've never seen the need to trust God. You're doing just fine as you are. Perhaps you've always enjoyed being a bit of a rebel or an 'independent spirit'. If so, I would encourage you to read on because

God has so much more for you than your current experience suggests.

Betrayal

We have all experienced betrayal of some kind. Most people who have been in leadership, in particular, will have been betrayed by someone close to them or let down by someone they believed they could trust, only to discover that this was not the case.

There will be people reading this right now who have been badly let down by those closest to them. My heart goes out to you. The very people you expected to be the most trustworthy have let you down and proved that they couldn't be trusted.

David understood this only too well:

"Even my best friend, the one I trusted completely, the one who shared my food, has turned against me" (Psalms 41:9, NLT).

Having been on the receiving end of this treatment on more than one occasion, I know exactly how it feels. The pain is deep and long-lasting. Our trust for others, never mind God ("how could He let this happen to me?") can quickly evaporate.

The Bible warns us against placing our confidence in men:

"Don't put your trust in human leaders. Don't trust in people who can't save you" (Psalm 146:3, NIRV).

It isn't just leaders who let us down, of course. Companies, employers, bosses, parents, children, siblings and even friends betray our trust. We live in a very broken world, and many of us have experienced some form of betrayal, broken promises, abuse, hurt, tragedy or loss.

Inner vows

It's possible you've been hurt so badly in the past that you've made an inner vow: "I will never, ever trust anyone again." I can understand this and I've made some similar vows to myself in the past. But none of them have been beneficial; they have only caused me more loss or harm in the long run. Can I encourage you to renounce any vows you've made before God and promise you'll trust Him wholeheartedly from now on?

Struggling to trust your own judgement
"The heart is deceitful above all things and beyond cure. Who can understand it?" (Jeremiah 17:9).

Have you ever spent time praying over a decision and eventually deciding on a particular course of action, only to discover down the line that you were completely wrong? I've been there several times in my family life and ministry. I rue those mistakes and poor decisions.

I believe another consequence of the fall is that the sinful nature battles with the spirit man. Sometimes our hearts yearn for things God doesn't want us to have. We must take care not to trust our own hearts, but to trust in God alone.

We have all made bad calls, been tempted, sinned and made the wrong choices, and the result is that we end up struggling to trust ourselves and our own judgement.

I've met several Christians over the years who have struggled to make simple decisions or take small risks purely because of past mistakes. They have been hamstrung by their past errors and are paralysed by the fear of making a mistake again. They also struggle to trust God with their lives and the future. I guess it's only natural that if we can't trust ourselves we will struggle to trust God and other people.

If you're one of these people, I pray that you will deal with the past. Bring it to your Father God in prayer and begin to take small steps of faith with His help. Don't allow the enemy of your soul to rob you of all that God has in store for you.

Whatever your reasons for not trusting God, the fact remains that He can be trusted. The Bible repeatedly exhorts us to trust Him. Why would a God who couldn't be trusted ask us to trust Him completely? There can be no half measures here. We either trust Him in every area of our lives or in none. In writing this book, my hope above everything else is that you will face down any particular trust issues you have and really learn to fully trust God. It will be so worthwhile!

Despite all the reasons why we may struggle to trust...

We were created to trust God

He wants us to trust Him deeply and unswervingly. In fact, I would suggest that God's desire is for us to have a wonderful, childlike faith, following the example of the little boy who offered his lunch (five loaves and two fishes) to Jesus. That's trust. The boy gave away his lunch knowing there were thousands of people to feed and that he was a long way from home. I bet he was starving, but something inside him said, 'Trust Jesus!' Imagine that. The boy's obedience provided the catalyst for a major miracle. Who knows what miracles your simple trust and obedience might produce?

In spite of your poor experiences and the untrustworthy people you have encountered, I would encourage you to place your trust in God again. He will never, ever let you down.

Getting started

Can I encourage you to take three steps towards trusting God and others? First, ask God to forgive you for any occasion when you haven't been trustworthy yourself, and have let people down. That's a good starting point. I'm sure I have let many people down over the years, and I am genuinely sorry for that.

Second, I would also encourage you to forgive those who have proven themselves unworthy of your trust. Give them a gift they probably don't deserve: the gift of forgiveness. It's hard to forgive at times. There have been several occasions when I have experienced great betrayal and disloyalty. However, we must begin to forgive for our own sakes. I've realised that the only person my unforgiveness impacts is me. My life, thoughts, behaviours, relationships, health and standing with God are all impacted, negatively and deeply, by my reluctance to forgive. But while I harbour unforgiveness, the other person is most likely getting on with his or her life, unaware that I am upset.

Why don't you stop reading for a moment and ask God is there is anyone you need to forgive? Make the decision to forgive that person now and verbalise it with your lips before your Father. I've learned that with major issues of forgiveness it helps to keep on forgiving whenever you have a flashback or memory of what has happened in the past. Eventually, you will find yourself completely free of the burden.

Once you have dealt with the unforgiveness, you will find it easier to trust again. You'll be released from the snare. The enemy of your soul has tried to entrap you, but you will walk away completely free of it.

I remember several years ago I was at a conference and we were encouraged to forgive those who had hurt us. It was really difficult, but I made the decision to forgive. As I did, my tears flowed freely for some time. Amid the freedoms God was bringing into my life, I felt Him whisper in my ear, "Simon, I will never allow anything as bad as this to happen to you again." That promise has stood me in good stead, especially in moments when I've begun to wonder whether it was all about to happen again. I believe this is God's promise for someone reading this book right now:

"My child, forgive those who have hurt and betrayed you, and My promise to you today is this: I will never allow anything as bad as that to happen to you again. Simply trust Me and begin to trust others again."

Third, ask God to restore in you a childlike faith like that of the boy with the loaves and fishes. He is the God who restores and rebuilds broken lives, so we can absolutely trust Him to help us in this.

Imagine

Now begin to imagine what your life could be like if you really started to trust God again, in spite of your experiences and the untrustworthy people you have encountered, and especially in those areas where you are struggling to trust Him right now.

Imagine the miracles that could happen in the areas of your life in which you are currently refusing to let God lead. As I said earlier, if we trust God like we never have before, we will live like we never have before.

Part II

Learning to trust

"Show me your ways, Lord, teach me your paths. Guide me in your truth and teach me, for you are God my Saviour, and my hope is in you all day long" (Psalm 25:4-5)

Chapter 3

Trust in the Lord

According to Christianity.com[ix], twenty-nine-year-old Jim Elliot had been looking forward to January 2, 1956, for several years. I imagine he arose quickly from his bed and completed his final preparations for the short flight across the thick Ecuadorian jungle. Several years of praying, planning and training had brought him and his four colleagues to this point.

In just a few short hours they would be setting up camp among an extremely dangerous and uncivilised Indian tribe known as the Aucas. This small tribe was renowned for killing all outsiders who ventured into their area. However, Jim and his friends knew that God had called them to go and share the gospel with this as-yet unreached people group.

Jim trusted God completely and, after a period of making simple connections with the tribe by way of gifts, the group decided to establish its base on a nearby beach. One by one, the team members were dropped off on the beach. However, within a few days, and after what had appeared to be friendly exchanges between the two groups, the five of them were attacked by a large group of Aucas with spears. They all died. Five women became widows that day, and nine children ended up fatherless.

However, that isn't the end of the story. Three years later, Jim's wife Elisabeth and his daughter Valerie, along with Rachel Saint (a sister of one of the men who had died), went to live among the tribe and shared the gospel with them. Many became Christians, and it is known as a Christian tribe to this day.

Jim Elliot had no doubt God that wanted him to tell the Aucas about Jesus. In fact, his trust in God was so deep that he felt willing to take the risk and begin to live among this dangerous people group. In his journal, he wrote: *"He is no fool who gives what he cannot keep to gain that which he cannot lose."*[x]

Thankfully, very few of us are called to such a challenging work as Jim. However, we are all called to trust God, and once we choose to do so I believe God will take us to places and create opportunities that we never could have imagined.

What is trust?
What do we actually mean by trust? The Oxford dictionary defines it as: *"Firm belief in the reliability, truth, or ability of someone or something."*[xi]

The Hebrew word for 'trust' is 'bâṭach', which has a primitive root. It literally means 'to hide for refuge'. Figuratively, it means 'to trust; to be confident or sure'. Trusting in the Lord with all my heart means to hide in Him for refuge, and to place *all my confidence* in Him.

Joshua trusted God. We see this throughout his time as the leader of Israel, and also in his final deathbed challenge to the people. As Joshua looked back to the conquest of the Promised Land, and forward to the future of the fledgling nation, he said this:

"But if you refuse to serve the Lord, then choose today whom you will serve. Would you prefer the gods your ancestors served beyond the Euphrates? Or will it be the gods of the Amorites in whose land you now live? But as for me and my family, we will serve the Lord" (Joshua 24:15, NLT).

Along with Joshua and many other biblical 'giants' (who we must never forget were ordinary people like you and me), Solomon learned to trust God for himself. Imagine how different your life would be if you really learned to do the same.

"If you grasp and cling to life on your terms, you'll lose it, but if you let that life go, you'll get life on God's terms" (Luke 17:33, MSG).

Who is this God in whom we trust?
If you've ever been to the US, you will probably have noticed the motto on the dollar notes: "In God we trust." This serves as a reminder to all Americans that trusting in God is the nation's ethos.

The history behind it is that the nation was facing a particularly tense time in 1956, during the Cold War, and the US wanted to distinguish itself from the Soviet Union, which promoted state atheism. As a result, the 84th Congress passed a joint resolution declaring "in God we trust" the national motto. The law was signed by President Eisenhower on the July 30, 1956, and the motto was progressively added to paper money between 1957 and 1966.[xii]

You may not agree with everything America does, but "In God we trust" should be the motto of every Christian.

"In you, Lord my God, I put my trust" (Psalm 25:1).

He is the God of Abraham, Isaac and Jacob! The children of Israel used this phrase to remind themselves who God was and what He had done. He is omniscient, omnipresent and omnipotent. He is the author, creator and sustainer of our universe.

It's so easy to forget who we are dealing with at times, or, better put, who is dealing with us. As we go about our daily lives, engrossed in work, family, bringing up children and generally making ends meet, we can easily forget who God is, and move away from that sense of awe and wonder.

JI Packer said: *"You don't get awe until you've begun to cultivate the sense that God is very great and you are very small."*[xiii]

As Rick Warren said: *"If God was small enough for you to completely understand him, he wouldn't be big enough for you to completely trust him."*[xiv]

Have you made God too small? Our God is the God of the universe; the one who created everything we can see and everything we can't. I could try to describe Him here, but He goes way beyond man's feeble attempts at description. If I've learned anything about Him, it is this: He never changes, and He is worthy of my trust. He has proven himself faithful again and again in my life. In fact, I've come to the conclusion that the ruler of the universe is on my side. He is *for* me and not *against* me.

I've learned to trust Him completely, even at times when it's been incredibly difficult and it felt as though God was unavailable, absent or disinterested. Without a doubt, this takes longer for some than others, and it begins with an initial choice to trust God. In many respects, trusting God needs to become like our trust of gravity. We know that gravity will never fail, and neither will our God.

"Those who know your name trust in you, for you, Lord, have never forsaken those who seek you," (Psalm 9:10).

Our help in ages past
The hymn, 'O God, Our Help in Ages Past' is sung at remembrance services the length and breadth of the land to commemorate those who have fought in wars. The hymn's title and theme are based on Psalm 90:1-2: *"Lord you have been our dwelling-place throughout all generations…from everlasting to everlasting you are God."*

These words were written by Moses as a prayer long before bombs and guns were created. Interestingly, 'O God, Our Help in Ages Past' was the last hymn to be sung on the Sunday morning aboard the Titanic[xv], and was also sung during Winston Churchill's funeral at St Paul's Cathedral in 1965.[xvi] It's a hymn that serves as a constant reminder, to our nation and to each one of us, of where our trust should be based: in God Himself, who has protected and rescued us and our ancestors through the ages.

"'To whom will you compare me? Or who is my equal?' says the Holy One. Lift up your eyes and look to the heavens: who created all these? He who brings out the starry host one by one and calls forth each of them by name. Because of his great power and mighty strength, not one of them is missing…Do you not know? Have you not heard? The Lord is the everlasting God, the Creator of the ends of the earth. He will not grow tired or weary, and his understanding no one can fathom" (Isaiah 40:25-28).

You can trust God because…
He is the truth, and His Word is the truth. He is totally consistent in all He does, and He has a great track record. He also tells us to trust him,

saying: *"Don't let your hearts be troubled. Trust in God, and trust also in me"* (John 14:1, NLT). Jesus also declared: *"...I am the way and the truth and the life..."* (John 14:6).

Revelation 19:11 (NLT) describes Jesus in this way: *"Then I saw heaven opened, and a white horse was standing there. Its rider was named Faithful and True..."*

I remember a season we went through about three years after we had been married. I had an amazing job, and Julia and I had just bought a beautiful new home together for our growing family. We were so happy. Then, out of the blue, my franchise contract was altered suddenly, without consultation, and pretty much everything I had worked for was stolen from me. Put simply, we could no longer afford the lifestyle we had created.

At the same time, the economy was in crisis, interest rates had hit the roof and we were financially crippled. It got to the point where I gave up my franchise as it wasn't worth running any longer. I became a humble egg delivery man instead. Yes, I drove a lorry and delivered farm eggs for a living. Unaware of our changed conditions, a neighbour thought Julia was having an affair with an egg man for a while! I gave up my nice car and cycled to work, where I would collect my lorry and delicate cargo. To say that it was completely humiliating is an understatement.

Even after making spending cuts, we were still in a massive mess. Our debts exceeded ten thousand pounds and the creditors were calling regularly. We were concerned at one point that we would lose our home altogether. Every which way we turned, there was no help. We spoke to bankers and lawyers, and tried everything and everyone, but there was no solution. In fact, every time we thought we had found a solution it turned out to be false hope. No help was available from anywhere.

I vividly remember worshipping God at church one Sunday, and we were singing "We Declare Your Majesty" (by Malcolm du Plessis). I sang those words, full of faith and trust, but the tears began to roll down my cheeks. At that moment, I could see no solution to our predicament. I saw even fewer signs of God's majesty or sovereignty in my life, yet paradoxically I totally trusted Him to come through for us. I really did. I just knew that I knew that I knew that He would. God had proved Himself faithful over the years, and I was certain that He wasn't about to start letting me down. And He did come through for us.

It was a really tough season, but we had to make the decision to *"...live by faith, not by sight"* (2 Corinthians 5:7). I continued riding my bike to work and delivering the eggs. The only benefit was that I was the fittest and thinnest I have ever been!

I discovered that day at church that deep trust often occurs in a place of complete weakness. It is possible to totally trust God during the toughest of seasons. God proved Himself faithful even during that horrendous time.

Steven Curtis Chapman sums this up well in his song, "My Redeemer is Faithful and True", and I would encourage you to read the lyrics for yourself. They remind us as we look back on the journey of life that Jesus is faithful and true, and will do everything He says He will do.

Trust His Word
Trusting God also means trusting His Word. I mentioned earlier that the devil has sought to deny the Word of God from the very beginning. When he challenged Eve's reasoning concerning the forbidden fruit, the devil replied, *"...You will not certainly die"* (Genesis 3:4). What God had made absolutely clear through His (spoken) Word, the enemy mocked and denied. Eve suddenly had a new perspective on the tree and was beginning to wonder how there could be any danger in eating that delicious fruit!

If we're really going to trust God like never before, we're going to need to ignore the question "Did God *really* say?" and learn to stand on His Word. His Word is truth (see John 17:17). What He says He does. When He makes promises He keeps them; whether that be to judge or to bless. What He declares will come to pass. His Word will never return empty or fail to accomplish His purposes (Isaiah 55:11).

I remember my mother saying to me as a young man that if God broke even one of His promises He wouldn't be God.

"...The Lord is trustworthy in all he promises and faithful in all he does" (Psalm 145:13).

Paul declares: *"If we are unfaithful, he remains faithful, for he cannot deny who he is"* (2 Timothy 2:13, NLT).

I have been unfaithful to God and let Him down many times during my journey of faith, but He has never, ever let me down. He has never failed to come through for me.

Trusting God like a king
When the Queen of Sheba heard of Solomon's fame, she couldn't resist paying him a visit. She arrived in Jerusalem with a large entourage and camels loaded with spices and large quantities of gold and precious jewels. On meeting Solomon she was overwhelmed by his wisdom and understanding. Nothing was too hard for the king to explain to her. She said:

> *Everything I heard in my country about your achievements and wisdom is true! I didn't believe what was said until I arrived here and saw it with my own eyes. In fact, I had not heard the half of it! Your wisdom and prosperity are far beyond what I was told. How happy your people must be! What a privilege for your officials to stand here day after day, listening to your wisdom!* (1 Kings 10:6-8, NLT).

Despite all his incredible achievements, Solomon had learned that the most important foundation for him as a king was to trust God. If we are going to succeed and prosper in life, we must learn how to trust like King Solomon. These wise words of his echo down the centuries:

"Trust in the Lord with all your heart and lean not on your own understanding; in all your ways submit to him, and he will make your paths straight."

The dreaded sickness bug

There have also been many times when I have stood on the Word of God because it was all I had. When we were at Bible college, we lived in a lovely flat on campus. During the autumn term, the whole family was struck down with sickness and diarrhoea. It was simply dreadful, and however hard we tried we couldn't stop the cross-contamination. The bug was starting to visit our four children and baby for a second time, and something needed to change!

While I'm not someone who blames the devil for everything, I sensed it was a spiritual attack and felt God telling me to stand on His Word. He gave me Psalm 35, and particular the first three verses:

"Contend, Lord, with those who contend with me; fight against those who fight against me. Take up shield and armour; arise and come to my aid. Brandish spear and javelin against those who pursue me. Say to me, 'I am your salvation'" (Psalm 35:1-3).

I started to pray these words around our flat that evening, asking God to fight on our behalf and praying that He would cleanse the apartment of all germs and bacteria. At about eleven thirty that evening the whole atmosphere changed. From that moment, everyone began to recover. God turned our darkness into light because we trusted His Word.

I have stood on the Word of God so many times and seen His provision. The one who has called you is faithful, and He will do it!

Flash floods

God has given us His incredible written Word in the Bible, but He still speaks to us today. I remember one evening I was walking my dog and talking to God about all our bills because I didn't know how we were going to pay them all. I felt the Holy Spirit, as He has so often done, whisper in my ear: "There are flash floods of blessings on the way!"

As I considered this, I realised God wasn't talking about a one-off blessing; rather, He was saying: "You're going to be flooded (yes, flooded!) with blessings, and these will take you by surprise and be ongoing." This comes directly from the Word of God:

You care for the land and water it; you enrich it abundantly. The streams of God are filled with water to provide the people with corn, for so you have ordained it. You drench its furrows and level its ridges; you soften it with showers and bless its crops. You crown the year with your bounty, and your carts overflow with abundance (Psalm 65:9-11).

I stood on this promise for some time, and over the following year we were blessed in so many unexpected ways. We received two large tax refunds, substantial gifts from preaching engagements, individual gifts to bless us, and holidays and trips abroad that were fully and unexpectedly provided for. God blessed us so greatly during that period. He is so good. As you can imagine, I stood on that promise for as long as I could!

This is why it's so critical that we read His Word every day. We need to know it so that we can stand on it. We also need to learn to hear and recognise His voice, and to stand on what He says.

In whom is your trust?
Julia and I love holidaying in Wales. It's one of the most beautiful and scenic places in Britain. A few years ago, we went to the Llŷn Peninsular in North Wales. Someone had told us about an old village, slate mine and coffee shop overlooking the sea in a remote place called Nant Gwrtheyrn. We were warned that the route down was very steep, but we decided to visit anyway.

When we got to the top of the hill and looked at the narrow road winding down the hillside, we looked at each other anxiously; Julia more than me, as I was the one behind the wheel. We decided to continue down this incredibly scenic route among the trees with a drop of several hundred to one side (I didn't dare look!). Eventually, with our hearts in our mouths, we made it to the bottom. I was glad my car had been fitted with new brake discs and pads a week before the holiday. Julia was just relieved to be alive. However, she had trusted me to get us to the bottom of the hill safely. Bless her!

Where is your trust placed? In whom or what do you trust?

King David stated:

"Some trust in chariots and some in horses, but we trust in the name of the Lord our God" (Psalm 20:7).

How did David learn this? Most of the kings of David's generation trusted in their armies. These soldiers were all they had to protect themselves in a primitive world. However, David was from a different mould. He had developed a deep dependency on God as a shepherd boy, looking after and protecting his father's sheep alone.

He initially learned to trust while fighting the lion and the bear, and this deep trust was also expressed when he tackled Goliath:

> *But David said to Saul, 'Your servant has been keeping his father's sheep. When a lion or a bear came and carried off a sheep from the flock, I went after it, struck it and rescued the sheep from its mouth. When it turned on me, I seized it by its hair, struck it and killed it. Your servant has killed both the lion and the bear; this uncircumcised Philistine will be like one of them, because he has defied the armies of the living God. The Lord who rescued me from the paw of the lion and the paw of the bear will rescue me from the hand of this Philistine.' Saul said to David, 'Go, and the Lord be with you'* (1 Samuel 17:34-37).

David fought many battles and faced many challenges to his kingship, but he had learned down the years to trust in one thing only: His God! A key verse in the Bible states this emphatically:

"It is better to trust in the Lord than to put confidence in man" (Psalms 118:8, NKJV).

Is your trust placed in someone or something rather than in God? Often we misplace it in our abilities, skills, bank balances, spouses or pastors; trusting anyone or anything other than God.

"Those who trust in their riches will fall, but the righteous will thrive like a green leaf" (Proverbs 11:28).

You may believe that you trust God, but is that really true? In my experience, it's easy to trust Him when life is going well and everything seems to be OK. However, it is when challenges and difficulties arise that we discover how much we really trust God.

It's little wonder that God on occasions allows the enemy freedom to challenge that trust, forcing us to depend on Him at times. Sometimes God will use difficult times as incubators of deeper trust. This was a lesson Job had to learn for himself.

"You will keep in perfect peace those whose minds are steadfast, because they trust in you. Trust in the Lord for ever, for the Lord, the Lord himself, is the Rock eternal" (Isaiah 26:3-4).

In which areas do you struggle to trust God completely?

In my experience, most people have at least one area of their lives in which they struggle to trust God. Sadly, failure to trust God as best we can in every area will only result in a lesser life. Why don't you pause for a moment and consider your own life? Is there an area in which you always seem to struggle to rely on Him? It could be money, career, relationships, family, ministry, health or your future.

I can almost guarantee that this distrust of God is mixed in with anxiety, fear and possibly bad experiences. The devil loves to develop these negative emotions, as he knows they will undermine our trust in God. I've tried to make it a policy never to entertain a thought that isn't from God.

As you look back on your life, is there much evidence that you depend on Him? God wants you to really trust Him. Imagine what He could do with your life if you chose to trust Him more.

Becoming more childlike

Our daughter Sarah was just five years old when she told us she wanted a bicycle like her friend Toni. The girls used to play together for hours in the Bible college grounds, but Toni had a beautiful bicycle and Sarah didn't. When she made her request, Julia said she would have to wait until Christmas if she wanted a bike, or she would need to pray and ask God for one.

As it was only September, Christmas seemed a long way off to Sarah, so she began to pray for the same bike. A day or two later, Julia bumped into a couple at the local Christian bookshop and was telling them about this. They said: "We have an old bike in our garage. She's welcome to it if you'd like it." I arranged to go and take a look on the Friday evening. That morning, Sarah woke up and said: "My bike's arriving tonight after dark." We hadn't told her at this point that I was going to look at one that evening as we were far from convinced that it would be anything more than a rusty old thing. However, Sarah had been praying.

Evening arrived, and I crept off to view the bike. To my utter amazement, it was exactly the same model as Toni's and in tip-top condition. It was the very bicycle Sarah has been asking God for. The only difference was that it had a stand, which she later said allowed them to tell the difference between the two.

I cannot tell you what joy and faith this incident brought Sarah as she excitedly cycled around the campus telling anyone who would listen how God had answered her prayer. In fact, the answer to prayer encouraged the whole student body because, on hearing of it, the college principal asked Sarah to share her faith story the next time they gathered together.

As I was pondering this, I remembered the words of Jesus:

Jesus called a little child over to him. He had the child stand among them. Jesus said, "What I'm about to tell you is true. You need to change and become like little children. If you don't, you will never enter the kingdom of heaven. Anyone who becomes as free of pride as this child is the most important in the kingdom of heaven (Matthew 18:2-4, NIRV).

Children are often completely trusting. They take God at His Word. We live in such a cynical and unbelieving world; a world that, if we allow it, will mould us into its ways (see Romans 12:2). Before long, we will become doubting and faithless, never expecting anything good to happen to us. Paul encouraged the Romans to be transformed by the renewing of their minds. I'm convinced that one of the greatest battles we face is to protect our minds. We must make every effort, with

God's help, to keep our thoughts positive, pure, faith-filled and deeply trusting.

I recently visited an old aunt who told me about an incident that happened when I was a little boy. I had a horrible itchy spot on my face when I was about four that wouldn't heal. When she asked me whether it was sore, I replied: "It's OK, Aunty. I've asked Jesus to help me not to scratch it, so I'll be fine." I want to be like that child again, with that simple faith in Jesus. Maybe just lately your circumstances have caused you to doubt and question your faith. Maybe you're struggling to trust God right now. Don't let that happen! Ask Jesus to give you faith like a small child again.

I guess we should also ask ourselves three questions at this point. First, if we're not trusting God in a certain area of our lives, whom are we trusting? Second, why are we not willing to trust God in this area? Third, do we honestly believe that we can look after it better than God?

Trust is like a compass, and God is at true north. If we allow ourselves to trust in someone or something else, even by just a small degree, ship captains would point out that we will eventually find ourselves thousands of miles away from our planned destinations. We may even find ourselves in danger of hitting the icebergs, whales, rough seas and rocks of life.

How can we really trust God?
To recap, here are my top tips for regaining your trust in God:

- Confessing where you haven't trusted him and asking for forgiveness.
- Forgiving those who have betrayed your trust (for example, spouses, bosses and friends), and declaring: "I will not allow what has happened in the past to stop me trusting God in the future!"
- Dealing with the times when God has appeared to let you down, or when prayers do not appear to have been answered.
- Relinquishing the inner vow that you will never trust God again.
- Surrendering your independent spirit.

- Relearning how to trust like a little child (see Matthew 18:3).
- Dealing with one thing at a time and taking every opportunity to trust. In every challenge that comes your way, make a choice to trust Him, and get back on the wagon quickly when you fail.
- Reading, knowing and standing on His Word. All His promises are yes in Christ Jesus (see 2 Corinthians 1:20). If you don't know what God has said, how can you possibly trust Him? Faith comes by hearing (see Romans 10:17).

But blessed are those who trust in the Lord and have made the Lord their hope and confidence. They are like trees planted along a riverbank, with roots that reach deep into the water. Such trees are not bothered by the heat or worried by long months of drought. Their leaves stay green, and they never stop producing fruit (Jeremiah 17:7-8, NLT).

Do you know Jesus Christ?
As I mentioned earlier, most of us will enjoy an average lifespan of more than twenty-five thousand days. No matter how many you have left, make a choice to trust Him today. The Apostle Paul wrote these incredible words:

"It's in Christ that we find out who we are and what we are living for. Long before we first heard of Christ and got our hopes up, he had his eye on us, had designs on us for glorious living, part of the overall purpose he is working out in everything and everyone" (Ephesians 1:11-12, MSG).

It's amazing to consider that the God of the universe had His eyes on us before we were born, and had designs on us for glorious living. Wow! How do we discover this new life? The Bible tells us that our sins and wrongdoing have separated us from a relationship with Father God, and that Jesus Christ died on a cross in our place so that we can know God once again for ourselves.

If you'd like to know Him for yourself, please pray this simple prayer:

Father God, I'm sorry for all the things I've done wrong in my life, and especially for the things I'm particularly ashamed of. I ask You to forgive me today, and to wipe the slate clean. Come and live in me by Your Holy Spirit. I surrender my life to You and make a choice that, with Your help, I will trust You and follow You all the days of my life. In Jesus' name, amen.

If you prayed that prayer and meant it, you've joined the worldwide family of God. You will not be disappointed. God has wonderful plans and purposes for your life. The important next step is to tell a Christian you know and join a Bible-believing church as soon as possible. Ask someone there if you can join a group where you can learn more about the Christian faith. I'm happy for you to contact me if you're struggling to find a good church.

Imagine

Imagine if you really had that simple childlike faith in God again. Why don't you make a list of the things that have caused you to stop trusting as you once did? Bring them before God in prayer and ask Him to prevent them from being stumbling blocks. Ask Him to restore your lost trust and to forgive you where you've trusted in yourself, someone or something else more than in Him, and make a fresh commitment to continue to trust in the Lord with all your heart. Begin to imagine where God might take you and ask Him to restore any broken dreams that you believe He placed in your heart.

Write a list of promises from the Bible that cover the areas where you struggle to trust God most (you can find these in some Bible editions or google them). Then stand on them every day. Place them somewhere prominent so you are regularly reminded of the ones you particularly need to focus on.

Chapter 4

What does trusting God with all your heart look like?

I once met a guy who I believe really trusted God. He was sold out for Christ, except for one thing. By his own admission, he simply could not trust God to take care of his children. What a tragedy. Those of us who are parents know how protective we feel about our children, but there comes a time when, for their own development and personal growth, we have to start letting go and trusting God to look after them.

Like the eagle rearing its young, we have to let them leave the nest. What is it that's holding you back? You may well be trusting God in almost every area, but in my experience very few Christians trust God implicitly across the board.

Abraham
Abraham is known as one of the 'heroes' of the faith. He was on a journey of faith and learning to trust God. It's easy to view his life and conclude that he had an amazing trust in God to the point that he was willing to obey God in sacrificing his son of promise on the altar. However, when we look more closely we see an ordinary man who, just like us, struggled at times to simply trust God.

At seventy-five years of age, Abraham followed the call of God to leave his land and people, and to trust God with his future. And yet he failed to trust God by pretending that Sarai was his sister and not his wife in Egypt. His lack of trust one day nearly caused a disaster the following day!

He trusted God in allowing Lot the more fertile land when they separated in the plains of the Negev. He trusted God by giving ten per cent of everything he had to Melchizedek (long before the Law demanded a tithe). But he failed to trust Him concerning the promise that he would be the father of nations, which resulted in the birth of Ishmael. He failed to trust a second time with Abimelech, again allowing the king to presume that she was his sister (he also placed his wife in a pretty difficult position!). Then he finally came good when God asked him to sacrifice his only legitimate son, Isaac, on the altar.

At ninety-nine years of age, Abraham trusted God when he was told that Sarah would have a baby, and that he would be the father of nations. You can't really blame Sarah for laughing! She was ninety years old. Imagine that! But God was true to His promise, and Paul records the great faith Abraham had in a bid to encourage us to really trust God:

> *Against all hope, Abraham in hope believed and so became the father of many nations, just as it had been said to him, 'So shall your offspring be.' Without weakening in his faith, he faced the fact that his body was as good as dead – since he was about a hundred years old – and that Sarah's womb was also dead. Yet he did not waver through unbelief regarding the promise of God, but was strengthened in his faith and gave glory to God, being fully persuaded that God had power to do what he had promised* (Romans 4:18-21).

There's a great summary of this in the final record of Abraham's story. I hope people will one day say this of me and you:

"And he died at a ripe old age, having lived a long and satisfying life. He breathed his last and joined his ancestors in death" (Genesis 25:8, NLT).

Abraham learned to trust God deeply, with all his heart. It was a journey, but it became the basis of his faith and the foundation for his hope. We must learn to trust God more. Failure to do so will cause us to miss out on the blessings, opportunities and experiences God has planned in advance for us.

> *Was not our father Abraham considered righteous for what he did when he offered his son Isaac on the altar? You see that his faith and his actions were working together, and his faith was made complete by what he did. And the scripture was fulfilled that says,*

'Abraham believed God, and it was credited to him as righteousness,' and he was called God's friend (James 2:21-23).

Solomon was the wisest man who ever lived

We would do well to not only take on board Solomon's wisdom, but to recognise that it came from a God who has a different perspective from our worldly perspective; whose ways are not our ways. Solomon had come to the realisation, as he considered his life, that really trusting God was the blueprint for successful living. He declared this God-inspired, God-breathed promise:

"Trust in the Lord with all your heart and lean not on your own understanding; in all your ways submit to him, and he will make your paths straight" (Proverbs 3:5-6).

I encourage you again to imagine how different your life would be if you really trusted God and lived out this oft-quoted verse in all its fullness and meaning. Imagine the impact on your faith, relationship with God and other relationships; on your marriage, children, finances, career, ministry, ambitions and dreams. Imagine what you could build or create with God if you really believed His Word. Imagine what He could do in and through you.

What does it mean to trust God with all your heart?

In the Bible, the word 'heart' is used figuratively and very widely for the feelings, the will and even the intellect; for the very centre of our being. Jesus said: *"...For the mouth speaks what the heart is full of."* (Luke 6:45).

Eventually, Abraham trusted God with every part of his being, will, feelings and intellect. The writer to the Hebrews recognised this wholehearted faith. He knew that Abraham was sure in the knowledge that, even if God required him to sacrifice his son, He could raise him from the dead.

By faith Abraham, when God tested him, offered Isaac as a sacrifice. He who had embraced the promises was about to sacrifice his one and only son, even though God had said to him, 'It is through Isaac that your offspring will be reckoned.' Abraham reasoned that God could even raise the dead, and so in a manner of speaking he did receive Isaac back from death (Hebrews 11:17-19).

Solomon encourages us to trust God; not in a half-hearted way, but with all our heart. This is what our faith in God demands. This life is certainly not for the faint-hearted!

John Wesley wrote: *"I saw, that giving even all my life to God...would profit me nothing, unless I gave... all my heart to him."*[xvii]

If you read the rest of Abraham's story, you will notice that, having been faithful in obeying God, he was blessed and trusted with even more.

Then the angel of the Lord called again to Abraham from heaven. 'This is what the Lord says: Because you have obeyed me and have not withheld even your son, your only son, I swear by my own name that I will certainly bless you. I will multiply your descendants beyond number, like the stars in the sky and the sand on the seashore. Your descendants will conquer the cities of their enemies. And through your descendants all the nations of the earth will be blessed—all because you have obeyed me' (Genesis 22:15-18, NLT).

Undivided heart

When we trust God, all goes well. When, we don't, and we take matters into our own hands like King Saul, the consequences can be serious:

'You have done a foolish thing,' Samuel said. 'You have not kept the command the LORD your God gave you; if you had, he would have established your kingdom over Israel for all time. But now your kingdom will not endure; the Lord has sought out a man after his own heart and appointed him ruler of his people, because you have not kept the Lord's command' (1 Samuel 13:13-14).

King Saul lost everything because he simply could not trust God. There is a lesson for us here that we would do well to heed. Saul wanted to depend on God but found himself torn at times, whereas King David knew the importance of trusting God with all his heart:

Teach me your way, Lord, that I may rely on your faithfulness; give me an undivided heart, that I may fear your name. I will praise you, Lord my God, with all my heart; I will glorify your name for ever. For great is your love towards me; you have delivered me from the depths, from the realm of the dead (Psalm 86:11-13).

A divided heart will always create distrust. If we're honest, we often trust God in the easier areas of our lives, for example:

- His forgiveness of us
- Salvation
- Eternity

However, we often struggle to trust Him with our:

- Finances and investments
- Careers
- Health
- Families
- Earthly future

God recognised that the hearts of the Israelites were divided:

'Therefore say: "This is what the Sovereign Lord says: I will gather you from the nations and bring you back from the countries where you have been scattered, and I will give you back the land of Israel again." 'They will return to it and remove all its vile images and detestable idols. I will give them an undivided heart and put a new spirit in them; I will remove from them their heart of stone and give them a heart of flesh. Then they will follow my decrees and be careful to keep my laws. They will be my people, and I will be their God' (Ezekiel 11:17-20).

There are so many places in the Old Testament where God tells His people how much He loves them and reminds them how much He cares for them, only for them to continually have their hearts drawn away by idols, heathen religions, worldly possessions and pleasures.

God repeatedly exhorts His people to have undivided hearts; hearts that love Him alone, trust Him alone and seek after Him alone. Like many of us today, they clearly struggled to do this, and their hearts were continually divided. They knew how they ought to live but struggled to live this way consistently. Yet God is constantly looking for people whose hearts are completely His:

"For the eyes of the Lord move to and fro throughout the earth so that He may support those whose heart is completely His..." (2 Chronicles 16:9, AMP).

Why is God looking for those whose hearts are totally committed to Him? So that He can support and strengthen them. How important is it to you that the Lord strongly supports what you are doing? If it's important, your heart must be completely His. When you embrace what is important to God, you bring your heart into alignment with His. When your heart is completely His, you will experience incredible grace and favour.

David
When David stepped out in front of Goliath, he demonstrated an undivided heart, and God supported him strongly:

David said to the Philistine, 'You come against me with sword and spear and javelin, but I come against you in the name of the Lord Almighty, the God of the armies of Israel, whom you have defied. This day the Lord will deliver you into my hands, and I'll strike you down and cut off your head. This very day I will give the carcasses of the Philistine army to the birds and the wild animals, and the whole world will know that there is a God in Israel' (1 Samuel 17:45-46).

David had already discovered that He could rely on God to deliver him from the lion or the bear, so this giant wasn't so terrifying. In God he put his trust. I wonder where your confidence is placed today. Have you learned to trust God completely? Baptist minister Charles Stanley said: *"Basically, there are two paths you can walk: faith or fear. It's impossible to simultaneously trust God and not trust God."*[xviii]

David chose to trust wholeheartedly and to step out in faith. This was one of David's prayers, and maybe it should be yours as you seek to trust the Lord with all your heart:

"Teach me your way, Lord, that I may rely on your faithfulness; give me an undivided heart, that I may fear your name" (Psalm 86:11).

Consider the faith journey God took David on as he sought to trust God with all his heart day after day. He learned to trust in smaller, less significant ways as a shepherd boy, which enabled him to take on the Philistine giant and ultimately to shepherd Israel as its king. David had no idea where his deep-rooted trust would lead at the point when his only concern was for the welfare of his father's sheep on the hillsides of Bethlehem.

If we will embark on our own unique journeys of trust, we may well be surprised where God takes us. I believe that, throughout history, God has been looking for men, women and children who will simply trust Him. As one of my friends used to regularly exclaim: "Lord, make me a doubt-free zone. Help me to trust you!"

Trust and the trellis

When I was a child, my parents were quite strict; even authoritarian at times. If we had a meal at my wonderful, godly grandfather's house, he used to pretend to be serious and say that we were only allowed to speak when he spoke to us. He was of the generation that upheld the old adage that children were to be seen and not heard!

Sadly, I had less and less respect for my parents and what they said as I grew up. I felt they were overly severe in their discipline, and that in many respects we were an inconvenience (I'm sure this wasn't true!). We were often sent to bed much earlier than our friends, who would be out in the street playing football under the streetlamps while

I watched longingly from my bedroom window. On one occasion I escaped and climbed down the wooden trellis so I could join them for a bit of street football. However, my return was somewhat hampered when the trellis collapsed. Try explaining that to an angry parent at the back door when you're supposed to be in bed!

I can clearly remember the frustrations and bad attitude I had during my early teens. I must have been the rebellious teenager from hell! Out of sheer frustration at the rule-ridden regime I was living under, I remember saying to my mother on my sixteenth birthday: "From now on, everything you say to me is advice." In other words: "I'm living my own way from now on, trusting my own instincts and not your rules!"

I guess I didn't really trust them at times because their outlook appeared old-fashioned. I wouldn't listen to or be guided by them; I just wanted to do what I wanted. I dishonoured them and refused to submit to them as parents, which was wrong, but I was pretty frustrated!

I've realised since then how important it is to respect and trust those whom God has placed in our lives. In fact, trust is actually an act of surrender and submission. Before we knew God, we were independent and in control of our own lives and destinies. But when we commit our lives to Him, we basically say: "I trust You enough to surrender to You."

Trust travels

Whenever we get in someone's car or on a plane, we're surrendering and submitting to the driver or pilot. We're silently declaring: "You're in charge now. I'm trusting you to get me to my destination safely." Imagine the dangers of trying to wrestle back control in a car or on a plane!

As American pastor and author, AW Tozer, said: *"The essence of surrender is getting out of God's way so that He can do in us what He also wants to do through us."*[xix]

I believe that our trust in God develops as we begin to surrender and submit our lives to Christ. Most of us felt we had done this when we first became Christians (and we might well have done at the time).

However, as the years have passed, many of us have created 'no-go zones' that remain un-submitted to Christ. Like my friend, we don't quite trust God to cover those areas. When we consider that for a minute, we realise how crazy it is! Is God's CV inadequate? Is He lacking in ability or experience? In recent years there have been several popular worship songs that talk about surrendering everything to Jesus. How easily we sing them without considering the vows we're making to God by singing those powerful words.

So where do we start? I believe this life of trusting God and discovering His amazing plan for our lives commences with a commitment to submission; making Jesus Christ Lord of all areas of our lives. Then it continues as a journey as He highlights the areas that we thought were surrendered but actually weren't.

I remember walking my dog and talking to my heavenly Father about our dream of owning our own home several years ago. I felt Him asking me to surrender this dream. I found myself praying, like the saints of old, "Father I have followed you since childhood, and whether you give us a home or not, I will follow you until my very last breath, come storm or trouble. I'm in!" Up to the present day, having made many sacrifices to follow God, we still don't own our own home. But, like Abraham, we absolutely believe that God will provide.

Surrender and submission must take place on a daily – moment by moment, situation by situation – basis. In my experience, there is a tremendous release when we do this. Gone is all the anxiety and pressure of controlling, managing and producing results in our lives. Instead, we find an incredible sense of peace and wellbeing. God is in control. Isn't this what Jesus taught?

"'Come to me, all you who are weary and burdened, and I will give you rest. Take my yoke upon you and learn from me, for I am gentle and humble in heart, and you will find rest for your souls. For my yoke is easy and my burden is light'" (Matthew 11:28-30).

Dr Paul Chappell writes:

> When D.L. Moody was just starting in the ministry he heard a preacher say, "The world has yet to see what God can do with a man fully surrendered to Him." Moody that night said, "By God's grace I'll be that man!" It is said that Moody shook two continents for God and over a million souls came to Christ under his preaching and ministry. Moody had little formal education, and he was not a polished speaker. But God greatly used his life.
>
> At a memorial service some years after Moody's death, Evangelist R.A. Torrey who had been one of his closest friends said, "The first thing that accounts for God's using D.L. Moody so mightily was that he was a fully surrendered man. Every ounce of that two-hundred-and-eighty-pound body of his belonged to God; everything he was and everything he had, belonged wholly to God."[xx]

When we completely surrender our lives to God, we rarely know what His plan is. Too many of us want to retain control. It would be great to be able to check out the plan first and then make a decision on whether or not it meets with our approval, but God gives no such option. He simply says: "Trust me and let me choose your path." Imagine what God might do with us if we are fully surrendered to Him.

My prayer is that someone who reads this book will grasp this point and respond with: *"By God's grace I'll be that (wo)man!"*

"It is out of our surrender that God can begin to use us and bless us" (AW Tozer).[xxi]

Trust relinquishes control

Trust involves putting God at the centre of our lives, rather than somewhere on the periphery. I used to play squash, and the aim of every good player is to control the match from the centre of the court. The question is this: is it you or God at the centre of the court in your life? There may well be a battle going on for that ground. My suggestion is that you make way for the King of Kings and Lord of Lords; the one who deserves and demands to be at the centre.

When we refuse to trust God with any area of our life, we retain control of that area. This limits God. While we dictate what happens, He cannot do anything. I've discovered that sometimes He will allow us to become 'god' in that area, managing and directing it ourselves without any help. He has no option but to withdraw and allow us to struggle. This might appear harsh but, like any parent, God wants us to learn life lessons. We need to learn to trust in Him and do things His way. I've lost count of the times when breakthrough has occurred when the centre-court-controlling Simon Lawton has stepped aside, chosen to trust God and allowed Him to do things His way.

Our church purchased the Dream Centre in July 2014, and since then we have been refurbishing it room by room, as and when funds allow. It's a massive project. We had an incredibly frustrating year in 2016 as money was tight and very little noticeable progress was being made. Such was my frustration towards the autumn that I actually said to God: "This is like the Israelites in Egypt. You're asking us to build your house without straw, never mind bricks!" In His gracious reply, God started to show me that my plans were not His because He has different priorities. He challenged me to relinquish control, revisit the order of works, get things in His order and take a step of faith.

Once I had submitted myself to Him and trusted His order of works, we almost immediately sold a building we had retained, releasing funds that completely covered the cost of the next stage He had directed. Following this, further funds started flowing in, allowing us to do even more than we had initially anticipated. When we fail to trust God, we miss out on all the resources of heaven He has made available for us.

Are there any areas of your life in which you are awaiting a breakthrough? Where nothing has changed, where there is no apparent solution and where you are frustrated by the lack of progress? Maybe you need to check yourself and surrender to Him, giving God full control. You may be surprised by the results!

Trust grows

We can't suddenly trust someone completely, and it's probably foolish to believe we can immediately trust God with every area of our lives, especially if we have been badly let down by others and our 'trust resources' are at an all-time low. Trust takes time.

Abraham grew in faith over the years. Can I encourage you to simply respond whenever He challenges you to trust Him in a particular area of your life? He is faithful to all His promises and loving to all that He has made (see Psalm 145:13).

Imagine

Imagine what God would trust you with tomorrow if you trusted Him more today. Abraham really trusted God and was blessed as a result. From Abraham to Paul, the narrative of the Bible is one of humanity learning to trust God. I'm absolutely convinced that God has our best interests at heart. He longs for our hearts to be undivided towards Him, trusting Him completely in everything. It starts with surrender and the relinquishing of control over our lives. This is where the battle rages. Imagine what God has in store for the man or woman who does this.

What are you withholding from God that He requires you to release back to Him? Imagine if you willingly released everything you hold dear. Imagine if you did what my friend was unable to do and were willing to release even your children to God. (In any case, they are already His and are only on short-term loan to us, as anyone with an empty nest will already have discovered.)

What is God speaking to you about right now as you read? What is it He wants you to trust Him with? Maybe it's something you used to trust Him in but somehow, through circumstances or a bad experience, you've lost your way and no longer do. Make a choice to trust Him from this moment on. Yes, stop and pray about this right now!

Prayer

Dear God, I'm sorry that trust has been an issue for me. I love You and am grateful for all You've done in my life, and I long to trust You more. Father, please take away every element of distrust I have in my heart. I ask You to forgive me and take me on a journey of trusting You more. Give me an undivided heart that totally depends on You. I offer my life to You afresh. You know what's best for me (and my family), so I gladly make the choice to trust You with every area of my life [name any area where you have struggled to let go]. Please give me assurance and peace that You have everything and everyone covered, and let my deep trust be the foundation of a strong faith in You. In Jesus' name, amen."

Chapter 5

Trust and Obey

I've sometimes wondered what it must have felt like to be Isaac the day he almost became the sacrifice on the mountainside. So often our focus is on Abraham's incredible willingness to sacrifice his precious son, but I'm pretty sure Isaac must have been wondering what the heck was going on at the time! There was no sign of a sacrificial lamb anywhere and, as Abraham gradually tied the boy up with ropes, Isaac, who could have resisted and run away, trusted his father and allowed himself to be laid on the altar.

By that point, I would have been thinking, if not saying: "Dad, what on earth are you doing? Don't you know that I'm your son, the child of promise?!" However, as Isaac lay there, I believe he trusted his father, and believed God would provide a sacrifice. Thankfully, just as Abraham was about to slay Isaac, the angel of the Lord shouted "Stop!" and a ram was provided.

Abraham was willing to sacrifice Isaac – the child he had waited an entire century for – if necessary. This is an incredible example of someone completely trusting God with all his heart. It seems crazy to us that Abraham would have even contemplated sacrificing his only son! It's quite difficult to believe that God tested Abraham in this extreme way. Maybe Isaac, his only child with Sarah, had become like an idol to Abraham. Who knows? All I know is that it was a tough test, and that Abraham passed it.

Abraham's trust was tested and challenged in the arena of complete obedience. Trusting with all your heart will always involve complete obedience to God.

Trust obeys

As a child at Sunday school, we used to sing what always seemed a somewhat cheesy song to me:

"Trust and obey, for there's no other way
To be happy in Jesus, but to trust and obey" [xxii]

It was a simple song, but it contained a powerful truth.

"It is not just trust; it is not just obey. It is trust and obey"
(AW Tozer).[xxiii]

We need to do both. In fact, we prove our overwhelming trust in God when we obey Him. When we disobey, we are emphatically stating that we think we know better! Surely obedience is a fundamental aspect of trust. We cannot claim to trust God if we repeatedly disobey Him and ignore His commands.

"All your commands are trustworthy..." (Psalm 119:86).

Trust is a recognition that God knows best, that His Word is truth, and that we're going to listen to Him, be guided by Him and allow Him to make the decisions. The longer I've been a Christian the more I've realised that God knows best. Not only is He trustworthy, but the guidelines and commands He has provided in the Bible are life-giving. They bring freedom and joy.

King David knew how critical it was to trust and obey God. He said:

"The law of the Lord is perfect, refreshing the soul. The statutes of the LORD are trustworthy, making wise the simple. The precepts of the Lord are right, giving joy to the heart. The commands of the Lord are radiant, giving light to the eyes" (Psalm 19:7-8).

"I take joy in doing your will, my God, for your instructions are written on my heart" (Psalm 40:8, NLT).

Throughout the Bible, God commands His people to trust and obey Him. The Old Testament is full of the covenant blessings of obedience (check out Deuteronomy 28:1-14 and Jeremiah 11:3-5, as examples).

Jesus Himself emphasised the importance of loving, trusting and obeying God:

"Jesus replied, 'Anyone who loves me will obey my teaching. My Father will love them, and we will come to them and make our home with them. Anyone who does not love me will not obey my teaching. These words you hear are not my own; they belong to the Father who sent me'" (John 14:23-24).

Living in responsive obedience

Just before Julia and I were married, an older and much wiser minister drew me to one side. He gave me the following verse of scripture:

"If a man has recently married, he must not be sent to war or have any other duty laid on him. For one year he is to be free to stay at home and bring happiness to the wife he has married" (Deuteronomy 24:5).

I had anticipated some powerful prophetic word that suggested I was the next 'man of power for the hour'. I can't say I was at all impressed by this verse! I was doing quite a bit of preaching in different churches locally at the time and was highly involved in serving at my home church. As you've probably guessed, I ignored this word from the Lord. I can only say that everything became much harder all of a sudden. Preaching preparation became really difficult and I didn't seem to be able to hear from God or receive a clear message from Him.

After several months, I succumbed to that wise advice in the Bible and took a year off from ministry. It was a lesson learned. I nearly missed out on a year of learning how to be a great husband and father because of my own disobedience and lack of trust in God. He knows best. We must choose to live our lives in responsive obedience.

Paul wisely wrote:

> *What I'm getting at, friends, is that you should simply keep on doing what you've done from the beginning. When I was living among you, you lived in responsive obedience. Now that I'm separated from you, keep it up. Better yet, redouble your efforts. Be energetic*

in your life of salvation, reverent and sensitive before God. That energy is God's energy, an energy deep within you, God himself willing and working at what will give him the most pleasure (Philippians 2:12-13, MSG).

During the Welsh Revival, Evan Roberts regularly preached a simple four-point message. It followed this pattern:
1) Confess any known sin to God and put away any wrong done to others
2) Put away any doubtful habit
3) Obey the Holy Spirit promptly
4) Confess Christ openly[xxiv]

I've decided that, as best as I can, I will trust and obey God as quickly as possible, without debate. That is trust. His commands aren't just perfect and trustworthy; they're also really good for us. We should trust God's advice and lifestyle laws. He knows best.

Don't say no!

During the final week of the Scottish independence referendum, Julia and I were enjoying a week's break in beautiful Perthshire. One day we visited the scenic village of Pitlochry. The YES and NO campaigns had positioned themselves at different ends of the main street, trying to persuade the local people how to vote.

As people walked down the road, there was a YES and a NO debate going on in their heads and hearts. It struck me how similar this is in our Christian lives. When God commands us to do something, we have our enemy, the devil, in one ear shouting, 'NO!' and the Holy Spirit gently encouraging us to say, 'YES!'

Someone once said that: "Every time we say no to God we are saying yes to the enemy of our souls." That's quite a sobering thought. I don't know about you, but as far as I'm able I want to respond quickly to the commands of God and the promptings of His Holy Spirit.

I suspect that some of us have become so used to saying no to God that we've forgotten how to say yes. When was the last time you said yes to God?

When my children were young, I would ask my daughter, who is a schoolteacher these days, to tidy her room. She would often reply, "In a minute", without having any real intention to tidy her room. (Incidentally, her room is no tidier now than it was back then!)

Over the years, I've heard my children repeatedly give that same reply, which always leads to inaction. You may smile at this, but how many of us say to God, "In a minute" and fail to follow through? Perhaps if we're honest, some of us never really have any intention of doing what God is asking.

The disappointing thing about this is that the breakthrough we are waiting for often lies on the other side of obedience to what He has clearly already told us to do.

If you remember the story of the miraculous feeding of the five thousand, it all started with a young boy's obedience to God. Whilst everyone else was starving hungry, I would have been tempted to disappear behind a rock and eat my lunch. However, this young man offered his five loaves and two fishes to Jesus, and an incredible miracle of provision followed. The other side of his obedience was an amazing miracle. Imagine the story that young boy had to tell when he got home: "Mum, you know that pack lunch you made me today…"

God loves, and blesses, obedience. He promises to bless us in all kinds of ways when we trust and obey. He just wants us to say yes!

If you listen obediently to the Voice of God, your God, and heartily obey all his commandments that I command you today, God, your God, will place you on high, high above all the nations of the world. All these blessings will come down on you and spread out beyond you because you have responded to the Voice of God, your God:

God's blessing inside the city,
God's blessing in the country;
God's blessing on your children, the crops of your land, the young of your livestock, the calves of your herds, the lambs of your flocks.
God's blessing on your basket and bread bowl;
God's blessing in your coming in, God's blessing in your going out.

God will defeat your enemies who attack you. They'll come at you on one road and run away on seven roads.
God will order a blessing on your barns and workplaces; he'll bless you in the land that God, your God, is giving you.
God will form you as a people holy to him, just as he promised you, if you keep the commandments of God, your God, and live the way he has shown you.
All the peoples on Earth will see you living under the Name of God and hold you in respectful awe.

God will lavish you with good things: children from your womb, offspring from your animals, and crops from your land, the land that God promised your ancestors that he would give you.
God will throw open the doors of his sky vaults and pour rain on your land on schedule and bless the work you take in hand. You will lend to many nations but you yourself won't have to take out a loan.
God will make you the head, not the tail; you'll always be the top dog, never the bottom dog, as you obediently listen to and diligently keep the commands of God, your God, that I am commanding you today. Don't swerve an inch to the right or left from the words that I command you today by going off following and worshiping other gods (Deuteronomy 28:1-14, MSG).

Trusting and obeying God doesn't mean that our lives will be perfect. However, I've discovered that God blesses us in all kinds of unexpected ways when we do. I absolutely believe that obedience opens the doors to God's blessing. In a sense, His hands are tied by our disobedience.

"No good thing does he withhold from those whose walk is blameless" (Psalm 84:11).

When we say no to God:

- We are saying: "I don't trust You!"
- We are resisting His will for our lives

- We are choosing a lesser life; missing out on His best life for us!
- We are undoubtedly missing out on blessings, new experiences, new levels of faith and deeper relationships

We should never underestimate what our willingness to obey can initiate. It's a catalyst for God's blessing in our lives. Remember, though, that obedience should flow from a deep love for God as our Father rather than from a desire for blessing.

We must remind ourselves that every time we say no to God we are allowing the enemy of our souls to rob us of the rewards our obedience to God brings. He alone knows what we miss out on every time we say no. Why would we withhold our obedience and deny ourselves or others His blessing?

God expects us to obey all His commands from scripture, but, like the young boy, He wants us to do what He has specifically told us to do, which might mean giving away our lunch (or something even more precious) at times! I have a suspicion that one of the reasons God granted King David so much favour in his life was that he desired to do all that God wanted him to do, precisely as God wanted him to do it.

"...I have found David son of Jesse, a man after my own heart; he will do everything I want him to do" (Acts 13:22).

Imagine what would happen if we responded more quickly to God. Imagine if we trusted God so much that we did everything He asked us to do. I'll say it again: if we trust God like we never have before, we will live like we never have before!

Making sacrifices

Abraham was willing to do something every parent would baulk at. He was willing to sacrifice his only son. Only God truly knows what that feels like.

As a boy, I used to attend the Pioneer Camp at Benllech Bay in Anglesey, North Wales. It's one of the most scenic areas in Britain and is still one of the places where I feel particularly close to God. David

Tryon, who led the camps back then, taught us about living for God. He said that in order to find our lives we had to be willing to lose them by offering them to God and trusting Him. He often quoted these challenging words of Jesus:

> Then Jesus said to his disciples, 'Whoever wants to be my disciple must deny themselves and take up their cross and follow me. For whoever wants to save their life will lose it, but whoever loses their life for me will find it. What good will it be for someone to gain the whole world, yet forfeit their soul? Or what can anyone give in exchange for their soul?' (Matthew 16:24-26).

These words gripped and challenged me. I wanted to find and enjoy life in all its fullness. I guess these verses have guided my entire adult life. Could they become life verses for you? Are you willing to set aside your dreams, ambitions and plans; to offer them to Christ in order to discover what He placed you on earth for? Are you willing to entrust your whole life to Him? Abundant living comes as a result of obedience, sacrifice, self-denial and a deep trust in God.

Julia and I have made many sacrifices to follow God. We've moved twice when the housing market has crashed. We are still recovering from the 2008 downturn, which happened just as we moved to our current church in Newcastle. That crash cost us our deposit and, as I said earlier, we still don't own our own home. Following Jesus and trusting God carries a high cost at times.

We left our four precious grown-up children (and subsequent grandchildren) behind when we followed God's call to move two hundred miles away from our existing home. We no longer see them every day as we used to. In fact, the distance means we have to stay over if we want to see them, and the demands of ministry mean it's difficult to see them as often as we would like. Your pastors may well have chosen to make this sacrifice in order to serve you and your local community, so try to encourage them. Remember that every time you see your family, your pastor and spouse are unlikely to be with theirs.

Trusting God requires self-denial at times, but Julia and I wouldn't want to be anywhere else in the world. God has given us a massive vision, amazing people and an incredible building through which to bring the love of God to our local community. We are completely at peace and content with where we are, trusting that He will come through for us and provide everything we need.

Trust Him with all your heart

I am repeatedly challenged by the words Paul used to remind the Corinthians of their status in Christ:

"...You are not your own; you were bought at a price..." (1 Corinthians 6:19-20).

While the context here is honouring God with our bodies, we must never forget the price Jesus paid for our salvation. Because of the cross, we have lost the right to do our own thing with our gifts and abilities, time and talents, opportunities and experiences, but why would you want to? Why would you choose to ignore God's plan for your life? His plans and purposes are far more fulfilling that anything we could dream up or imagine, and they're tailored precisely to your life. We were bought at a high price, so let's make sure we live our lives according to His plans and purposes. We will never, ever regret it.

Trials and challenges

Like you, I have moments of doubt and distrust when I know God is asking me to do something that is going to involve a high personal cost. A battle begins to rage in my mind as I try to decide whether to obey God or do my own thing.

Sometimes we can struggle to trust Him when a trial seems to go on and on without any end in sight. That's so hard. I've been there. In fact, I believe the toughest situations are the ones that we have absolutely no control over. That's when we have to really trust God.

You might have received some bad news, be facing impending redundancy, suffer from health problems, be experiencing financial difficulties, or have family or relationship issues. In my fifty-plus years I have faced most of these in some form or another. However, God has proved Himself faithful and true every time. Can I encourage you to bring these struggles to God right now? Why don't you pause a moment and pray and entrust Him with them completely?

"But blessed are those who trust in the Lord and have made the Lord their hope and confidence. They are like trees planted along a riverbank, with roots that reach deep into the water. Such trees are not bothered by the heat or worried by long months of drought. Their leaves stay green, and they never stop producing fruit (Jeremiah 17:7-8, NLT).

I'm praying that as you read these words you will be encouraged and filled with renewed confidence. I hope you will make the decision not to quit, but rather to trust God even more deeply. Never forget that it is possible for your life to be fruitful even in the darkest of times.

Imagine

God really wants us to learn to trust Him fully and to prove this through responsive obedience. At times this will involve sacrifice. Let's make a decision to say yes to God more often. We'll never regret it! There are tremendous promises in the Bible for those who say yes. When we say no we're only harming ourselves and limiting our lives.

Ask God to highlight any areas in the past where you've hurt Him by failing to say yes, or worse still where you've made Him a vow or promise and failed to follow through. Then ask Him to help you trust and obey Him more today than yesterday.

Chapter 6

Stop worrying!

J. Arthur Rank, an English executive, decided to do all his worrying on one day each week. He chose Wednesdays. When anything happened that gave him anxiety and annoyed his ulcer, he would write it down, put it in his worry box and forget about it until next Wednesday. The interesting thing was that the following Wednesday when he opened his worry box, most of the things that had disturbed him six days earlier were already settled. It would have been useless to have worried about them.[xxv]

Why do we worry so much? From my own experience being a Christian doesn't make you immune to worry and anxiety. The apostle Paul encouraged the believers in Philippi not to worry:

"Don't worry about anything; instead, pray about everything. Tell God what you need, and thank him for all he has done" (Philippians 4:6, NLT).

Paul identified a problem here that so many of us face. Instead of trusting God, we worry. As Christians, we shouldn't worry. It's the opposite of trust.

Very few people worry about nothing at all. Some worry about absolutely anything and everything, and I mean everything. In fact, when things in their lives are going well, they begin to worry that there's nothing to worry about!

Maybe you're worried about one of the following concerns right now:

- Your own health, or the health of a loved one
- Money, debt or retirement income
- Relationships (romantic, or with family and friends)
- Job security and work pressure

- Growing old
- Physical appearance
- What other people think of you

Five hundred years ago, French philosopher Michel de Montaigne said: *"My life has been filled with terrible misfortune; most of which never happened."*[xxvi]

In recent years, studies have shown that many of our imagined calamities never actually materialise. An article I read[xxvii] cites one particular piece of research in which people were asked to write down their worries over an extended period of time and identify which of their imagined misfortunes didn't happen. The researchers discovered that:

- Eighty-five of the subjects' main worries never manifested
- Of the fifteen percent that did, seventy-nine percent of subjects discovered they were able to handle the difficulty in a better way than expected, or found that the difficulty taught them a lesson that was worth learning.

This means that the majority of what we worry about is nothing more than a fearful mind punishing you with exaggerations and misconceptions.

Worry impacts our health
The stress hormones released into our brains due to worry have been linked to:

- Shrinking brain mass and memory loss
- Reduced IQ
- Depression
- Sleeplessness
- Weight gain
- Greater risk of heart disease and cancers
- Premature ageing and dementia

The word "worry" comes from an old Anglo-Saxon word meaning "to choke" or "to strangle".[xxviii] That's a very apt description of what worry does to us. It's little wonder that it can have such a powerful impact on almost every area of our lives.

Worry impacts our relationships, as we're present and yet absent, and our creativity and reasoning, as it's very difficult to be creative or problem-solve when our minds are elsewhere. It disables us, destroys our faith, and increases our fear and anxiety levels. Worry is not good for us.

Take back control
Somehow, we need to regain control over the worries that habitually, incessantly and often unconsciously take hold of our minds. If we could become like air traffic controllers of our minds and stop those worrying thoughts landing, I believe we would greatly increase the odds of living longer, happier, peace-filled and successful lives.

Make a choice
Why don't you make a choice today that, with God's help, you are not going to worry about anything from now on? Instead, you're going to trust God completely.

As American preacher and author Joyce Meyer said: *"When we pray and then worry, we are not exercising trust in God. We are not fully releasing our burdens or needs to Him; we are 'taking them back' and working them over in our minds."*[xxix]

I've heard people say: "My mum/dad was a great worrier, so I am too." This suggests that it has been inherited through our genes. Can I suggest that this is a lie planted by your enemy, the devil? Cast that lie off and make the choice to live worry-free. God has called you to be a warrior, not a worrier!

Antidotes for worry
Philippians is one of my favourite epistles and in it Paul suggests several antidotes to worry, including the following.

Always be full of joy in the Lord

"Always be full of joy in the Lord. I say it again—rejoice! Let everyone see that you are considerate in all you do. Remember, the Lord is coming soon" (Philippians 4:4-5).

We should be the most joyous people on earth! Joy is a fruit of the Spirit. It comes from:

- Knowing God
- Understanding who we are in Christ
- Appreciating our eternal destiny
- Being content with what we have in any given circumstance (see Philippians 4:11-13)

Be considerate of others

"Do nothing out of selfish ambition or vain conceit. Rather, in humility value others above yourselves, not looking to your own interests but each of you to the interests of the others" (Philippians 2:3-4).

We can get so wrapped up in ourselves, can't we? When we begin to worry, one of the best things we can do is look to the needs of others. When I say to Julia, "Sweetheart, what can I do today to take the pressure off you? How can I help, babe?" this not only makes her feel loved and cared for, but it also helps me stop worrying about my problems and focus on making her life better. (She hates being called 'babe', by the way. That was just for emphasis!)

Be thankful!

"...thank him for all he has done!" (Philippians 4:6, NLT).

Sometimes we forget how much we have, and all that God has done in the past. When I look back I remember so many answered prayers, breakthroughs, provisions, blessings and healings. I'm reminded that God is on my side; that He hasn't forgotten me, even if He doesn't always do things my way. I find that encouraging. He's never early or late, but always on time. And even in the darkest days He is there. So many of the things I wasted time worrying about never came to pass, and when they did God either delivered or helped me through.

Pray about everything!
Paul exhorts us to talk to God about everything we are concerned about. Everything means everything!

"Don't worry about anything; instead, pray about everything..." (Philippians 4:6, NLT).

Peter encourages us to:

"Cast all your anxiety on him because he cares for you" (1 Peter 5:7).

Don't allow anything to worry you. Trust God and pray about everything! Make a decision to leave everything that concerns you with Him.

As American author Max Lucado says: *"No one can pray and worry at the same time. When we worry, we aren't praying. When we pray, we aren't worrying."*xxx

I've discovered that the more I bring my day, my plans, family, concerns, stresses and pressures to God, the more He works in my life. Praying and releasing my day to Him each morning makes an incredible difference to the way the day goes. He often surprises me, and the day is often easier, or help is offered, or deadlines are extended, or appointments are cancelled.

Tell God what you need
"And my God will meet all your needs according to the riches of his glory in Christ Jesus" (Philippians 4:19).

Just recently, we were doing some evangelism in a local park and I noticed a young man who I thought at first was drunk as he kept leaning forward and almost falling to the floor. I realised after watching him for a few moments that he was looking for something. It turned out that the previous night he had lost a silver pendant from around his neck. Not only was it valuable (£400), but it had been given to him by a family member. He was distraught.

As I listened to him, I felt God remind me that He supplies all our needs. God said: "Pray with the boy that I will show you where it is." So I did, and we continued to search the whole area where he had been. It was the middle of a sunny day, and I naturally began to wonder whether someone had seen the glint of silver earlier in the day and picked it up.

However, I kept looking with this young guy. Suddenly, I felt God guide me to look in a different area near some railings about ten feet outside the 'search area'. Something glinted in the sun, and there it was. I held it up and shouted to him, "Is this what you're looking for?" The guy was absolutely ecstatic! He couldn't stop thanking me and hugging me and smiling. I said to him: "Never forget that God is real. Forget me, but always remember that He found your pendant today, and that He promises to meet all your needs if you will only ask Him."

That story still makes me smile. I love what God did for that young man, and I hope he never forgets it. It really illustrates that there is no need to worry. It's so much better to trust God and pray. You see, our greatest needs cannot exceed God's limitless resources! The more I pray, the more God intervenes. The more I pray, the more miracles He does. The more I pray, the more peace I have and the better I sleep. Paul encouraged the believers to: "Tell God what you need." Many times, God has not only met my needs, but has provided above and beyond what I had expected.

Guaranteed answers to prayer

Do you think there are any ways to guarantee that your prayers will be answered?! I've put together a list of things that give us favour with God.

Good credit at the prayer bank

If God had a bank account containing our prayers, what would your balance be right now? Are some of us guilty of constantly overdrawing? Maybe our accounts are in the red. I honestly believe that nothing benefits our lives more than praying, and that when we pray we build up a balance in our favour. The conclusion I've come to in my life is this: if I will trust God, live to please Him and put His Kingdom first (particularly in prayer), He will look after the things that concern me. If prayer was a bank account, would yours be in credit?

Right motives

"You desire but do not have, so you kill. You covet but you cannot get what you want, so you quarrel and fight. You do not have because you do not ask God. When you ask, you do not receive, because you ask with wrong motives, that you may spend what you get on your pleasures" (James 4:2).

It's important to have the right motives as we pray. Having said that, God is my Father and I'm not afraid to ask Him to bless me. Jabez asked God to bless him. He said:

"...'Oh, that you would bless me and enlarge my territory! Let your hand be with me, and keep me from harm so that I will be free from pain.' And God granted his request" (1 Chronicles 4:10).

So often we hear Christian leaders talk about God being able to meet our needs, but I believe that God is like any good father. He loves to bless His kids, so He responded to Jabez's prayer by blessing him. God didn't need to bless him or enlarge his territory, but He chose to bless His child. I've learned from this that I should never be afraid to ask God to bless me beyond my simple everyday needs, and consequently I've seen Him provide for holidays, date nights, bikes, caravans and trips abroad. He's a good, good Father.

Wise requests

Sometimes we simply ask for the wrong things. We think we know what's best for us – that promotion, new car or romantic relationship – but we might be surprised one day to discover some of the heartache we missed out on without achieving them.

Clean living

If we want God to answer our prayers, we should make every effort to live in the right way.

"If I had cherished sin in my heart, the Lord would not have listened; but God has surely listened and has heard my prayer" (Psalm 66:18-19).

"Dear friends, if our hearts do not condemn us, we have confidence before God and receive from him anything we ask, because we keep his commands and do what pleases him" (1 John 3:21-22).

I believe God purposely withholds from us sometimes because He wants to get our attention. A question I occasionally use in sermons is this: "Have you done what I've told you to do?" I believe it's one that God would ask some of us today.

Great expectations

Scottish minister Andrew Murray taught this:

> *Each time, before you intercede, be quiet first, and worship God in His glory. Think of what He can do, and how He delights to hear the prayers of His redeemed people. Think of your place and privilege in Christ, and expect great things! Beware in your prayers, above everything else, of limiting God, not only by unbelief, but by fancying that you know what He can do. Expect unexpected things 'above all that we ask or think.*[xxxi]

There is so much to think about in that quote. As we learn to trust God more, it's critical that we learn to pray more effectively. Deep trust married with effective prayer changes situations. Imagine what God could do if we really learned to trust Him when we prayed.

Lay it out before the Lord

Have you ever received a letter or an email containing bad news? Perhaps you were informed of health problems, poor exam results, a credit refusal or the death of a friend. We could learn a great deal from

King Hezekiah. He received a threatening letter from Sennacherib, the Assyrian King who had already attacked and captured all the fortified cities of Judah, and Jerusalem was next on his hit list. The letter basically said: surrender or die.

Hezekiah laid the letter out before the Lord (see 2 Kings 19:14-19) and prayed. He was willing to humble himself before God and acknowledge his dependency on Him. As a result, God promised Hezekiah that He would deal with the Assyrians. That night, the angel of the Lord put to death a hundred and eighty thousand men in the Assyrian camp. The people woke up to find dead bodies everywhere, and a day later Sennacherib was assassinated by his sons while worshipping at his temple. God can dramatically change a situation within twenty-four hours!

There have been several times in my life when I've knelt down and laid the threat out before the Lord. There is something powerful and releasing in completing this simple act and appealing to God as Hezekiah did. As you lay your situation out before God you are:

- Acknowledging your own helplessness and dependency on God
- Bringing it before the Lord of Lords and King of Kings
- Humbling yourself under God's mighty hand that He might lift you up
- Releasing a burden to God, saying: "I am not going to worry about this any longer." (Pressure is released, and you instantly feel better.)
- Connecting your situation to the same power of God that supernaturally rescued Israel from the Assyrians

During 2017, our church received a massive business rates bill of £36,000, and we appealed it for more than a year. Eventually, the authorities reduced it to just under £14,000, which was still a lot of money, and money we simply didn't have. We laid the invoice before the Lord prior to appealing again and prayed that He would deal with it. The council changed its mind a few days later and relinquished us from all further business rates!

On every occasion that I have felt it right to lay something before the Lord, God has come through for me. Maybe you have just received some bad news. Let me encourage you to lay it out before the Lord. As you pray, be faith-filled and expectant that the same God who rescued Hezekiah will also rescue you.

The peace of God
In the meantime, the promise of God is that if you choose not to worry about anything and pray about everything:

"Then you will experience God's peace, which exceeds anything we can understand. His peace will guard your hearts and minds as you live in Christ Jesus" (Philippians 4:7, NLT).

It's a wonderful promise that when we've chosen to pray about everything God's peace will fill us, guarding our hearts and minds against further worry.

A footnote in the NIV says that the peace of God is not *"merely a psychological state of mind, but an inner tranquillity based on peace with God…The opposite of anxiety, it is the tranquillity that comes when the believer commits all his cares to God in prayer and worries about them no more".*[xxxii]

The Greek word for 'guard' comes from the military word 'garrison'. God posts a sentry to stand guard over our minds in a very real sense. His protective custody extends to the core of our being as we choose not to worry but rather to trust Him and pray.

Imagine
We must learn to stop worrying about so many things, trusting Him and praying about everything. We must determine to be warriors, not worriers. So often the devil will use the same people or situations to cause us anxiety.

How many times have you been worried about an aspect of your health only to see a headline about it on the news or in the paper? (The devil is naughty!) Determine now that you will, with God's help, trust Him and not worry. Pray that every time you're tempted to worry

He will remind you to simply come to Him and experience His peace. Then press on and enjoy your day and the people around you. Don't not let the enemy rob you of life for a second longer. Is there anything you need to bring to God in prayer right now?

Consider starting a trust journal and write down all the things you struggle to trust God with. Begin to entrust them to Him every day and record what happens. You will be surprised!

Chapter 7

Don't lean on your own understanding

"Have you never heard? Have you never understood? The Lord is the everlasting God, the Creator of all the earth. He never grows weak or weary. No one can measure the depths of his understanding" (Isaiah 40:28, NLT).

You've probably never heard of Buckminster Fuller. He created the 'Knowledge Doubling Curve' when he noticed that, up until 1900, human knowledge had approximately doubled every century. By the end of World War II, it is thought that knowledge was doubling every twenty-five years.[xxxiii]

Today, things are not quite as simple, because different types of knowledge have different rates of growth. For example, it is said that nanotechnology knowledge is doubling every two years and clinical knowledge every eighteen months. Average human knowledge is doubling every thirteen months. According to IBM, the impact of the internet will eventually lead to the doubling of knowledge every twelve hours.

Humanity has become so clever! Never has a generation had so much knowledge, yet lacked so greatly in understanding and wisdom. We are ever-seeing and ever-hearing, but rarely understanding.

Our understanding changes
As our knowledge grows, so does our understanding. What we once believed to be correct or true may since have been proven wrong. Take a look at some of this past understanding, as recorded by Human Science:[xxxiv]

"The horse is here to stay, but the automobile is only a novelty—a fad." (Advice from the president of the Michigan Savings Bank to Henry

Ford's lawyer, Horace Rackham. Rackham ignored the advice and invested $5,000 in Ford stock, later selling it for $12.5 million.)

"There is no likelihood man can ever tap the power of the atom" (Robert Millikan in a 1923 speech to the Chemists' Club in New York).

"[Television] won't be able to hold on to any market it captures after the first six months. People will soon get tired of staring at a plywood box every night" (Darryl Zanuck, head of 20th Century-Fox, 1946).

"Rail travel at high speed is not possible because passengers, unable to breathe, would die of asphyxia" (Dr Dionysius Lardner, professor of Natural Philosophy and Astronomy at University College London).

"This 'telephone' has too many shortcomings to be seriously considered as a means of communication. The device is inherently of no value to us" (Western Union internal memo, 1878).

It's incredible how our knowledge and understanding has grown and developed over the last hundred years or so. And yet this pales into insignificance compared with God's understanding.

His understanding
There are some pretty intelligent people in our world! In fact, there are many people around the world with an IQ exceeding two hundred, and some with two hundred and twenty plus. In the UK, the average is one hundred and four.

However, there are even better brains in our world, including guys such as physicist Stephen Hawking and chess player Gary Kasparov. In fact, Kasparov drew a game against a computer that could process three million positions per second in 2003. But if we combined all that thinking and brain power, it wouldn't even touch on God's understanding of His world.

Then the Lord spoke to Job out of the storm. He said: 'Who is this that obscures my plans with words without knowledge? Brace yourself like a man; I will question you, and you shall answer me.

'Where were you when I laid the earth's foundation? Tell me, if you understand. Who marked off its dimensions? Surely you know! Who stretched a measuring line across it? On what were its footings set, or who laid its cornerstone— while the morning stars sang together and all the angels shouted for joy?

'Who shut up the sea behind doors when it burst forth from the womb, when I made the clouds its garment and wrapped it in thick darkness, when I fixed limits for it and set its doors and bars in place, when I said, "This far you may come and no farther; here is where your proud waves halt"?

"Have you ever given orders to the morning, or shown the dawn its place... Have you journeyed to the springs of the sea or walked in the recesses of the deep? What is the way to the abode of light? And where does darkness reside? Have you entered the storehouses of the snow or seen the storehouses of the hail, which I reserve for times of trouble, for days of war and battle?' (Job 38:1-12; 16; 19; 22-23).

God's understanding is off the scale compared with even the most intelligent human understanding. His understanding is beyond our comprehension.

Oh, the depth of the riches of the wisdom and knowledge of God! How unsearchable his judgments, and his paths beyond tracing out! 'Who has known the mind of the Lord? Or who has been his counsellor?"

'Who has ever given to God, that God should repay them?' For from him and through him and for him are all things. To him be the glory forever! Amen (Romans 11:33-36).

God's knowledge is indescribable. He is all-seeing, all-knowing, all-powerful and present everywhere. He is infinite, immortal and unfathomably wise. Part of trusting God with all our hearts is to depend on His wisdom rather than relying on our own limited viewpoints.

"But God made the earth by his power; he founded the world by his wisdom and stretched out the heavens by his understanding" (Jeremiah 10:12).

Simply put, we must learn to trust Him rather than leaning on our own understanding.

Don't let the world shape your understanding
"Do not be shaped by this world; instead be changed within by a new way of thinking. Then you will be able to decide what God wants for you; you will know what is good and pleasing to him and what is perfect." (Romans 12:2, CEV UK).

Paul warned the Roman believers not to allow the world to shape their understanding, but rather to be renewed by the transforming of their minds. I suspect that very few of us realise how influenced we are by worldly values and thinking.

First, we must first learn to trust with our whole hearts. Second, we must avoid depending on our limited understanding because:

"'My thoughts are nothing like your thoughts,' says the Lord. 'And my ways are far beyond anything you could imagine. For just as the heavens are higher than the earth, so my ways are higher than your ways and my thoughts higher than your thoughts'" (Isaiah 55:8-9, NLT).

We must recognise that God has a clearer understanding than us and depend on His wisdom rather than our own if we are to walk down straight paths and experience life in all its fullness. Imagine what our lives would be like if we really grabbed hold of this. We would live like we never have before!

Depending on our own understanding
Are there any areas in which it is OK to depend on our own understanding? I would suggest that we don't need to ask God about

anything He has clearly revealed in scripture or about the minutiae of daily living, such as:

- Which clothes to wear (although that might help speed up the process for some of us!)
- What to make for breakfast
- Whether to have a latte or a mocha
- Whether to purchase low-value items or not

However, there are some areas where we should certainly depend on God's understanding:

- Major decision making, for example exams, universities, careers, relationships, homes, relocating and investments
- When trials and difficulties arise. As international advocate for people with disabilities Joni Eareckson Tada said: *"True wisdom is found in trusting God when you can't figure things out."*[xxxv]
- When we fail, or appear to have failed
- When someone attacks us, or we make an enemy
- When things don't work out as we anticipated

I remember being interviewed for a manager's job at a retail store in Bridgwater, Somerset, during my early twenties. I felt I had conducted a near-perfect interview, and the panel confirmed this. However, I wasn't offered the position because they selected an internal candidate. As you can imagine, I was absolutely gutted and couldn't understand why God hadn't intervened and given me the job.

However, six months later I was appointed to the same position in Wisbech, where God straightened me out and called me to ministry. I probably wouldn't be where I am today, or have met Julia, if God hadn't made my paths straight. He always knows best. His ways are not our ways, so we mustn't depend on our own limited understanding.

"Those who trust their own insight are foolish, but anyone who walks in wisdom is safe" (Proverbs 28:26, NLT).

So what *shouldn't* we do?

Don't follow hunches, gut feelings or emotions
I believe we need to be really careful with our thinking. As Presbyterian minister, Dr Frank Crane, once said: *"Our best friends and our worst enemies are our thoughts."*xxxvi

Even as I write this chapter, I'm working through some challenges with people and constantly asking God: "Is my thinking on this godly? Have I got this right? Is this how you see this situation?" I've discovered that it's easy for me to see things the wrong way or to misinterpret depending on all kinds of exterior and interior circumstances. When I'm busy, tired, listening to the wrong people (or even the enemy himself, who loves to sow seeds of doubt, discord, criticism and judgement, and loves to inflate small issues) and thinking negatively, my attitude can be all over the place.

I need to constantly check that I am fixing my thoughts on what is *"true, and honourable, and right, and pure, and lovely, admirable...Things that are excellent and worthy of praise"* (see Philippians 4:8, NLT). My constant prayer is that I will see people and situations as He sees them.

I've also discovered that my independent spirit will often try to direct me towards a human solution rather than a spiritual one.

American journalist HL Mencken said: *"There is always a well-known human solution to every human problem – neat, plausible, and wrong."*xxxvii

The world teaches us to trust our own intuition or 'gut feeling'. It tells us, "If it feels good. Do it!"

American psychologist and TV personality, Joyce Brothers, said: *"Trust your hunches. They're usually based on facts filed away just below the conscious level."*xxxviii

Canadian singer Bryan Adams said: *"I've only ever trusted my gut on everything. I don't trust my head, I don't trust my heart, I trust my gut."*[xxxix]

When we get a 'gut feeling' about things, we are relying on our senses, intellect and experience. However, Eve was deceived when she relied on her senses; King David committed adultery and murder when he trusted his gut instinct; King Josiah was killed in a battle he never needed to fight (we can also be drawn into battles we never needed to join!); and Samson thought it would be OK to get a haircut!

Jesus came that we might have life, but the enemy of our souls comes to steal, kill and destroy (see John 10:10). Too many lives have been messed up and ruined by people following hunches or going with their gut feelings. While our feelings change, the Word of the Lord stands forever.

Here's what the Bible says:

"Leave your simple ways and you will live; walk in the way of insight" (Proverbs 9:6).

We need to be people who don't depend on our own understanding, which is fallible, weak and changeable. Our hearts can also be deceitful at times. We need to trust God and depend on His understanding. He knows things we don't, and remember this: He sees the future.

Don't rush!

Slow down and take your time. There is rarely any rush to make a major decision or to spend a lot of money. I learned this lesson the hard way a few years ago. I was so keen to book into a conference in Phoenix, Arizona, that I felt I needed to get the flights booked quickly and make sure everything was arranged many months in advance. I didn't pray about it, and a week after booking the flights and hotels the conference was suddenly moved to LA. I wasn't happy! Changing my travel arrangements cost a lot of money and created a lot of hassle. Why didn't I wait a little longer? Why was I in such a rush? Why didn't I consult God?

Don't react or overreact

Our responses in the heat of the moment aren't usually good. I wonder how many of us have, in the past week, said something we shouldn't have, pressed send on an unwise email, rushed into an unnecessary and costly commitment, or reacted in the midst of an apparent storm, only to realise that if we'd only waited it would have died down.

American pastor and author, TD Jakes, said: *"Never make a permanent decision based on a temporary storm. No matter how raging the billows are today, remind yourself, 'This too shall pass.'"*[xl]

Don't judge

We lean on our own understanding when we judge others and situations from a worldly perspective. Several years ago, I did just what Samuel tried to do when he 'prayerfully' looked for a successor for Saul. He looked at the outward appearances rather than at the heart.

At the time, we needed to urgently replace one of our important volunteer team leaders. I chose a guy who I got on well with and knew quite well, and who I thought would be great. Eighteen months later, I had lost most of the team; a very talented group of people. It took us years to recover what was lost by my poor (and not-prayed-through-enough) decision. David enquired of the Lord before he made major decisions. I didn't, and I paid a high price, as did my church.

It is also possible to make judgements on people when they let us down, make a mistake or do something we disagree with. Have you ever done this, only to realise later that there were particular reasons (often acceptable) why they chose that course of action.

Jesus taught us: *"Do not judge, or you too will be judged"* (see Matthew 7:1). There is such wisdom in this. We lean too easily on our own understanding when we judge, and we mustn't forget that there is only one true Judge. Next time you're tempted to judge, ask yourself these questions:

- Do I know all the facts and the background?
- Do I know why they did it; what their motives were?

- Have I put myself in their shoes?
- Do I know what they know?
- Have I prayed about it, or am I being tempted to make a snap judgement?

Let's remember to treat others as we would want to be treated ourselves.

Don't try to figure it all out

Elim leader David Campbell said: *"Sometimes when we want to experience the peace that passes all understanding, we need to give up our right to understanding."*[xli]

We can easily waste valuable hours trying to figure things out or anticipate outcomes rather than committing the matter to God in prayer. I'm not saying we shouldn't think things through with God's help and seek solutions, but I've found that I have the ability to go way over the top and waste days of creative thinking time on just one matter. It's not God's will for us to be so measured about this.

I have literally wasted hours analysing people, situations, threats and challenges down the years. Hours and hours have been thrown away trying to anticipate what would happen, what someone had actually meant by what they said, what they might do next, what I should do next, and so on. It's fruitless. I've had sleepless nights trying to lean on my own understanding. Dwelling on something you can't change is a pointless exercise. God wants our minds to be used more productively.

What if you 'figure it all out', and then God surprises you and does something different (and much better)? You've wasted all that time thinking through all the various scenarios and outcomes. Every second we waste worrying, we are preventing our minds from receiving God thoughts and ideas, which could transform our lives, homes, churches and careers. Your worrying could actually stop you receiving an inspirational idea! Let God carry the load and choose to live like you never have before. He already has everything under control and mapped out, so just trust Him.

What should we do?
Rather than leaning on our own understanding, what should we do?

Pray, pray, pray!
That's how we "acknowledge Him", as Proverbs 3:5-6 urges us to do. We're talking to Him; asking for His wisdom and greater understanding. It can be as simple as: *"I don't get this, Lord."*

By doing this, we're acknowledging that our own understanding is limited, and that we need His understanding in every decision we make.

> *Seek the Lord while he may be found; call on him while he is near. Let the wicked forsake their ways and the unrighteous their thoughts. Let them turn to the Lord, and he will have mercy on them, and to our God, for he will freely pardon. 'For my thoughts are not your thoughts, neither are your ways my ways,' declares the Lord. 'As the heavens are higher than the earth, so are my ways higher than your ways and my thoughts than your thoughts'* (Isaiah 55:6-9).

I would encourage you to really soak any important decision in prayer. Nothing will benefit you more. This is what it means to trust God. When you acknowledge God in every important decision you make, you are giving Him permission to lead, speak, guide, direct and give wisdom. On the contrary, when you fail to pray you are saying, "I know best." What a tragic thought that is.

Consider
I mentioned earlier the dangers of dwelling on something for too long. However, we do need to spend some time considering the way forward in certain situations, just as long as it doesn't completely occupy our thoughts, conversations and lives.

My father, who was an engineer, taught me a valuable lesson during my younger years. If something broke in our house – for example a door mechanism – he would say: "First of all, examine it closely. Never force it into place or make it do something it shouldn't. When you've spent time examining it, next spent some time considering how it was designed to work, and how it could be repaired."

If only I had applied this to my own life more often. There is so much wisdom and understanding in living like my engineer father. How often we rush straight in, trying to make things happen or forcing a certain result without pausing to think, reflect and consider the matter in full. Sometimes we need to give our issues some devoted thinking time.

One of the most important leadership lessons I've learned is to give things time.

"The simple believe anything, but the prudent give thought to their steps" (Proverbs 14:15).

As American author John Maxwell said: *"Our lives today are a result of our thinking yesterday, and our lives tomorrow will be determined by what we think today."*[xlii]

Imagine the outcomes in your life if you spent a little more time considering your ways. People talk about needing to 'sleep on it', but I encourage people to 'week on it'. That allows us to give major decisions time, and also gives God time to intervene or speak.

Know what God has already said
God went to a lot of effort to give us something on paper. The Bible took several thousand years to put together, and God inspired every word of it for our benefit. People sacrificed their lives to get it in print, so why do we ignore it? I try to read it first thing every day. Yes, before I check my social media accounts and the news. His Word is sweet and offers incredible wisdom:

"How sweet are your words to my taste, sweeter than honey to my mouth! I gain understanding from your precepts; therefore I hate every wrong path. Your word is a lamp for my feet, a light on my path" (Psalm 119:103-105).

"The unfolding of your words gives light; it gives understanding to the simple" (Psalm 119:130).

> *My son, if you accept my words and store up my commands within you, turning your ear to wisdom and applying your heart to understanding— indeed, if you call out for insight and cry aloud for understanding, and if you look for it as for silver and search for it as for hidden treasure, then you will understand the fear of the Lord and find the knowledge of God. For the Lord gives wisdom; from his mouth come knowledge and understanding. He holds success in store for the upright, he is a shield to those whose walk is blameless, for he guards the course of the just and protects the way of his faithful ones. Then you will understand what is right and just and fair—every good path. For wisdom will enter your heart, and knowledge will be pleasant to your soul. Discretion will protect you, and understanding will guard you* (Proverbs 2:1-11).

If you read His Word regularly, you will be amazed at how often God speaks to you in the midst of major decision-making, and in everyday occurrences.

Seek the counsel of others
"Plans fail for lack of counsel, but with many advisers they succeed" (Proverbs 15:22).

In my second year at Bible college, I was offered the pastorate at an attractive church in the Manchester area with a good salary. I was flattered. We were broke and it certainly stroked my ego. However, after discussing this with the college principal I came to the correct conclusion that it was not the right move for me. Looking back, I wasn't ready for the cut and thrust of pastoral ministry. More importantly, I had gone to college to learn, and I still had a couple of important years to complete.

The interesting thing is that the principal allowed me to consider it, pray it through and take time to make my decision. When I let him know my decision, he told me he was delighted. He also informed me that hadn't wanted to influence my decision as he had been considering me for an important role at the college, which he then offered me. I was asked to be chairman of the students for the next academic year.

Whatever age we are, I believe it's important to have people around us who we can go to for wise counsel. They need to be people who are godly and are willing to be honest with us. We gain nothing from people who simply stroke our egos and agree with us, but we gain massively from those who have trodden the path before us and can help us learn from their mistakes.

US naval officer, Admiral Hyman Rickover, said: *"It is necessary for us to learn from other people's mistakes. You will not live long enough to make them all yourself."*[xliii]

Before the days of satellite navigation, it was often quite hard to find a specific address in an unknown area. How many of us (especially men, apparently!) have driven around for hours, to the frustration of our women folk, and refused to ask for directions. The choice to slow down the process by asking for advice or seeking wise counsel is foreign to many of us. Like the Israelites, we loathe doing it, but God instructs it:

"This is what the Lord says: 'Stand at the crossroads and look; ask for the ancient paths, ask where the good way is, and walk in it, and you will find rest for your souls.' But you said, 'We will not walk in it'" (Jeremiah 6:16).

It's important to seek wise counsel at times, but some of us:

- Never ask anyone for advice and counsel (bad idea!).
- Spend all our time asking others and no time seeking God.
- Have a tendency to spend too much time listening to people who haven't earned the right to speak into our lives; advisors who have leaned too much on worldly understanding and sometimes have selfish motives.

The question is: whose voice influences you most? Whose voice *should* influence you most?

Let's ask the question another way. When you make a decision, whose reaction do you worry about first or most? I would suggest that this person possibly has too much influence in your world.

If we had listened to the advice of some friends, Julia and I would never have got married. We would never have left Leicester for Bible college. We would never have planted a church, led two Christian camps, relocated to Newcastle or purchased the Dream Centre. None of this would have happened if we had listed to the 'wise counsel' of some people we spoke to.

Please take care. Some people have selfish motives, and they may possess ungodly wisdom. They lean on the world's understanding. We were told: "You can't go to Bible college because you haven't rented out your house. You have no money, no grant and no financial support." Yet God used that experience to stretch and build our faith. Even though it looked crazy to others, God was in it.

"As the Scriptures say, 'I will destroy the wisdom of the wise and discard the intelligence of the intelligent'" (1 Corinthians 1:19, NLT).

Is there a 'significant other'; a person in your life who you listen to more than God? If so, I would encourage you to address this as soon as possible.

Take the 'peace' test

When making major decisions, I believe that we need to have a certain amount of peace. That doesn't necessarily mean we are a hundred percent at peace about every element of the situation. I don't believe that ever happens. However, I do believe that as we grow and mature in our relationships with God, we develop a 'sense of knowing' that something is the right thing to do.

Once we've done 'due diligence', as they say in the business world – once we've played our part in asking God to guide us and listened to godly counsel – I think the moment comes when we have to make a decision. At that point, we check our hearts and consider whether we feel 'at peace' with the situation. Sometimes we might choose to delay for a little longer just to be sure. There have been times as senior pastor when my elders have felt sure about something and I've needed a little longer to be absolutely sure.

I believe that God grants us peace once when we've done due diligence and have heard from Him correctly. That's what I look for.

"You will keep in perfect peace those whose minds are steadfast, because they trust in you. Trust in the Lord forever, for the Lord, the Lord himself, is the Rock eternal" (Isaiah 26:3-4).

Obey God

At times it comes down to this: trust and obey. Sometimes God will ask us to do something that looks crazy in the world's eyes and maybe even in our own.

Naaman the leper had it all worked out. He would meet the prophet Elisha, who would either lay hands on him or send him a handkerchief he had prayed over, and the leprosy would disappear (see 2 Kings 5:12).

Elisha didn't even go out to meet this mighty centurion. Instead, he sent a message: "Go take a dip in the Jordan seven times." The Jordan was a pretty filthy river at that time, and Naaman's reaction was equally bad:

> *But Naaman went away angry and said, 'I thought that he would surely come out to me and stand and call on the name of the Lord his God, wave his hand over the spot and cure me of my leprosy. Are not Abana and Pharpar, the rivers of Damascus, better than all the waters of Israel? Couldn't I wash in them and be cleansed?' So he turned and went off in a rage* (2 Kings 5:11-12).

We know the rest of the story. Eventually after listening to his servant girl, he went and bathed in the Jordan, as directed by Elisha, and was subsequently healed of leprosy.

I guess we need to be careful in every situation not to try to impose our own thoughts, expectations and wishes, but rather to carry our precisely what God has instructed us to do. Otherwise, we risk missing out on God's best.

Just recently at the Dream Centre we were attempting to refurbish the proposed new coffee shop, and the finances simply weren't flowing. I started to seek God about this and He made it clear that the coffee shop was not his priority (many of us struggled with this!), and that we should start refurbishing another area. We obeyed and, while we don't yet enjoy great coffee (that will have to wait), a whole new area of the centre has been refurbished. God provided. We're still learning not to lean on our own understanding.

Never forget
We rarely (if ever) have the full picture. Our own understanding is simply not enough to lean on. God has the full picture. He is omniscient. He knows all things.

The wisest people, and certainly the wisest leaders, have learned to ask God for His thoughts, which are always fully informed, and His ways, which are always better ways than our ways. They have learned to listen, grasp issues, consider different viewpoints and not to rush in like fools. They ask the right questions to discover, learn and depend on God's greater wisdom and knowledge.

I once had a friend who would jump in with a response before listening and getting the full picture. He used to infuriate me! I would try to share with him a particular situation I was dealing with at church and the different angles, but before I had been given time to explain much he had already made a snap statement or judgement. I'd be thinking, "Hang on, I haven't finished telling you everything yet!"

Make sure you're not like that friend. Don't leap in with advice before you have understood the bigger picture.

For we know in part and we prophesy in part, but when completeness comes, what is in part disappears. When I was a child, I talked like a child, I thought like a child, I reasoned like a child. When I became a man, I put the ways of childhood behind me. For now we see only a reflection as in a mirror; then we shall see face to face. Now I know in part; then I shall know fully, even as I am fully known (1 Corinthians 13:9-12).

God wants us to trust Him with all our heart and not to lean on our own understanding. He wants us to get this. These words of wisdom could save you a lot of heartache and pain. Ask yourself again: whose understanding am I trusting, and who am I going to trust from now on?"

Imagine
"Discretion will protect you, and understanding will guard you" (Proverbs 2:11).

So often we lean on our own understanding and, because we have been conditioned by the world around us to expect very little from others and God, we forget to dream or imagine. Yet we serve a God who is incredibly creative, and who desires to work in and through us for His purposes. The limited understanding we have of our own abilities often causes us to accept the very minimum for our lives rather than expecting God to do more.

"Now to him who is able to do immeasurably more than all we ask or imagine, according to his power that is at work within us, to him be glory in the church and in Christ Jesus throughout all generations, for ever and ever! Amen" (Ephesians 3:20-21).

Why not take a moment to ask God to refresh your understanding and to replace it with His immeasurable understanding? Say to Him: "Lord, I don't want this old way of thinking for a second longer. I want to be renewed by the transformation of my mind."

Imagine if He became the biggest influence in your life rather than you relying on your own limited understanding of yourself, your abilities and your limitations? If you began to really trust Him with your life, imagine what He would entrust you with in the future. Imagine if you gave God permission to take hold of your life, ambitions and dreams. Imagine the adventures, dreams and experiences you might have with God doing the steering and the hard lifting. Imagine what your life could be like tomorrow if you trusted God more today.

"I'm enough of an artist to draw freely on my imagination, which I think is more important than knowledge. Knowledge is limited. Imagination encircles the world" (Albert Einstein).[xliv]

Chapter 8

In all your ways acknowledge Him

Trust God from the bottom of your heart; don't try to figure out everything on your own. Listen for God's voice in everything you do, everywhere you go; he's the one who will keep you on track. Don't assume that you know it all. Run to God! Run from evil! Your body will glow with health, your very bones will vibrate with life! (Proverbs 3:5-8, MSG).

In all your ways

Most people have a morning routine or ritual. I get up at around five or five thirty and stick the kettle on in order to wake me up, as I like to start the day with God. The first drink of the day simply has to be tea. I'm English, so please make allowances for this. My second cup is always coffee ("Thank goodness," some of you are saying). This has been my ritual for some forty years, so nothing is going to change it now. My wife's routine is that the first two cups of the day are tea. If these don't materialise, let's just say Julia finds it a little more difficult to get up!

Apparently, the older we get the more set in our ways we become. Some people suggest that once we hit our late twenties it's actually difficult to break some of those set habits and routines.

So what does it mean for us to acknowledge God in all our ways? Does it mean we have to involve Him even in simple decision-making, such as whether to have tea or coffee as our first drink of the day? I believe that we need to grasp the depth of meaning of this phrase in the original text. The Hebrew word for 'ways' is 'orach', which means "a customary path or a well-trodden road". The picture is similar to that of a cattle path; a path of mud from the pasture to the milking barn, worn down from repeated travel, day after day after day. Figuratively, it describes a way of living or a mode of action.

We are to acknowledge Him in our everyday lives and in the major decisions we make. Every day as we travel down the familiar paths of our lives, we must make sure we are travelling towards Him, communing with Him and fully involving Him.

If you enjoy reading different versions of the Bible, you will have noticed that Proverbs 3:5-6 has been translated in slightly different ways, which helps us grasp their full meaning.

We are told to:

- Acknowledge Him (KJV)
- Seek His will (NLT)
- Submit to Him (NIV UK)
- Let Him lead us (CEV)

Acknowledge Him
Every day, you will have brief passing conversations with people that go something like this:

"Hi mate. How are you doing? You OK?" Often we don't even wait for a response.

I suspect that God is suggesting a little more than a passing acknowledgement in our relationship with Him. I am concerned that so many Christians do little more than pay lip service to this primary relationship. Involving Him in our day-to-day lives and decisions is quite a rare occurrence for some. This results in decisions being made with little consultation of the One who knows all things: past, present and future.

Now listen, you who say, 'Today or tomorrow we will go to this or that city spend a year there, carry on business and make money.' Why, you do not even know what will happen tomorrow. What is your life? You are a mist that appears for a little while and then vanishes. Instead, you ought to say, 'If it is the Lord's will, we will live and do this or that.' As it is, you boast in your arrogant schemes. All such boasting is evil. If anyone, then, knows the good they ought to do and doesn't do it, it is sin for them (James 4:13-17).

"God, bless our plans!"

We cannot expect to simply inform God of what we've already decided to do at the last minute and then ask Him to bless those plans. Some people claim they want to be guided by God, but the reality is they want God to fit into their plans. If they pray at all about their latest relationships, plans or schemes, it is almost always to ask or demand that God blesses those decisions.

It is far better to discover what God's plans are and then get on board with Him, which will guarantee success. But that's challenging and time-consuming because you will have to spend time asking Him in the first place.

No more bailouts

Recent bank bailouts angered many of us because the banks' mistakes cost ordinary taxpayers a lot of money, and there appeared to be little or no accountability. However, the bankers are not the only ones who have made poor decisions at times.

A couple of years ago, I bought a car that I had test driven some time back and had always wanted. It was a Nissan X-Trail 2.2. It was awesome, and I loved driving the big beast. Unfortunately, my dream car had many mechanical problems in the two years I owned it, culminating in the engine blowing up without warning as I returned home from church one day! Added to this, it drank a lot of diesel (and I mean *a lot*). It was an impulse buy that I hadn't consulted God about, and I was relieved to eventually swap the dream car for something newer and more economical that I actually had prayed about.

How many of us have invested in property, bought cars or changed jobs on a whim, only to later discover that it wasn't a good idea, never mind a God idea! Sometimes we get so excited about an opportunity that we impulsively jump in with both feet, failing to even mention it to God. Occasionally we may 'run it past him' to belatedly seek His blessing. I guess most of us are guilty of this.

But God desires to be involved more in our daily lives. He knows what's best for us and longs to guide us along paths that will benefit us, His children. Like any father, He wants more than a cursory acknowledgment each day and delights in being more involved in the important decisions in our lives.

We pay lip service when we make major decisions, then expect God to bail us out when it all goes pear-shaped. As I look back, there have been several occasions when I've asked God to get on board with my plan, investments or church vision, and then when it has gone wrong I have had to appeal to Him for help. God perhaps needs to say to one or two of us: "No more bailouts!"

Wisdom says we need to do more than just quickly 'acknowledge' Him. Most of the time when we acknowledge someone, we simply greet them as we walk past or confirm that we've received a text, email or delivery. Our relationship with God must go deeper than this; it really must. A minimal acknowledgment is not enough when we're talking to Him about our hopes, dreams, plans and ideas.

If we are claiming to really trust in the Lord with all our heart, this must be reflected in the way we live and make major decisions.

Getting to know God

How can you better acknowledge Him? The primitive root of the word translated as 'acknowledgement' is 'yada', which means 'know'. The same word is used in Genesis where Adam "knew" Eve and she conceived (see Genesis 4:1, KJV). There is a deep sense of knowing God within a committed covenant relationship, and consequently this verse requires far more than simply acknowledging Him in our decisions. There is also a sense of knowing Him well and understanding what He desires.

When you really know someone, you know what they like and want. In a marriage, you soon get to know the person and with time you get to know almost intuitively what they would say, do or choose in any given situation.

Get to know Him

The word 'yada' is used again in Hosea 6:3, where the exhortation is to "acknowledge the Lord" and "press on to acknowledge him". This is expressed so much more clearly in the *Amplified Bible*:

"So let us know and become personally acquainted with Him; let us press on to know and understand fully the [greatness of the] Lord [to honour, heed, and deeply cherish Him]."

I believe there are two clear aspects to this type of knowing God. First of all, we must recognise who He is. We can so easily forget who we are dealing with and bring Him down to our feeble, inadequate human level. In *Knowing God*, JI Packer reminds us of the magnitude of difference between us and the God we seek to know:

> *Today, vast stress is laid on the thought that God is* personal, *but this truth is so stated as to leave the impression that God is a person of the same sort as we are – weak, inadequate, ineffective, a little pathetic. But this is not the God of the Bible! Our personal life is a finite thing: it is limited in every direction, in space, in time, in knowledge, in power. But God is not so limited. He is eternal, infinite, and almighty. He has us in his hands; but we never have him in ours.*[xlv]

For me, this quote acts as a constant reminder that God is completely different from me. This creates a desire in me to know this incredible God and Father in a much deeper and more intimate way. I can only imagine what my life would be like if I got to know Him even better.

The second aspect of this acknowledgment of God is developing a sense, through relationship, of knowing what God wants. When we truly know God, we should almost instinctively know what He would want us to do. That doesn't mean we should never seek Him at all. This will always be necessary when making important decisions. However, the more we know God the more likely we are to sense what His will is.

We discover God's plans and purposes through spending time with Him in fellowship; by reading His Word and praying. There is no substitute for time spent alone with God. I have learned that it is far better to uncover His plans and get on board with them than to try to do it the other way around. This is something Israel never really grasped:

'Woe to the obstinate children,' declares the Lord, 'to those who carry out plans that are not mine, forming an alliance, but not by my Spirit, heaping sin upon sin; who go down to Egypt without consulting me; who look for help to Pharaoh's protection, to Egypt's shade for refuge. But Pharaoh's protection will be to your shame, Egypt's shade will bring you disgrace' (Isaiah 30:1-3).

As theologian John Gill puts it in his *Exposition of the Old and New Testament*: "Have him always in view; consider him as ever present with thee, observing every step thou takest; and take not one step without his leave."[xlvi]

This must always be our objective.

Let Him lead

The Message puts Proverbs 3:6-7 like this: *"Always let him lead you, and he will clear the road for you to follow. Don't ever think that you are wise enough, but respect the Lord and stay away from evil."*

I like that. Along the journey called life, always let Him lead you in all your ways. Maybe this is a good moment to pause for thought and consider who is leading you right now. The Bible encourages us to be led by the Holy Spirit, and to keep in step with Him. So often we are led by our own thoughts, ideas and gut feelings, or by 'influential others' in our lives, for example family members, friends and colleagues. Surely our greatest desire should be to always let Him lead us. If we do so, we will experience the best outcomes in life. Imagine the synergy that occurs in connecting our lives with Him. The result is that incredible favour, blessing and power is released.

"Oh, that we might know the Lord!' Let us press on to know him. He will respond to us as surely as the arrival of dawn or the coming rains in early spring" (Hosea 6:4, NLT).

If we will allow Him to lead, He will surely lead us along straight paths.

Decide not to decide until He decides

People say that the older you get the more you realise how little you actually know. I've certainly come to that conclusion. God knows it all, so I've made the decision to acknowledge Him in all my ways, and also that I won't decide until He decides.

I've discovered that sometimes I can hear from God and be on the right track, but the timing isn't quite right. For instance, just recently we were planning to move closer to the church and started viewing properties, but no doors appeared to be opening. I just sensed that the timing was wrong, so we've stopped looking until we feel prompted by Him to start again.

American author Eugene Peterson wrote: *"Waiting in prayer is a disciplined refusal to act before God acts."*[xlvii]

I've learned to pause and pull back, knowing that if God wants me to go down that route there is absolutely no rush. He will open the door at just the right time, so I can sit back and wait. The flip side, of course, is that He may not actually want me to move, or He might want me to wait for His very best, which may not be available yet. Trusting God with all my heart means slowing down sometimes and believing that He is always right.

The race is not 'to the swift'

It seems to me that we are always in a rush to make decisions, but the Bible is clear that the fastest runner doesn't always win. We need to slow down.

> *I have observed something else under the sun. The fastest runner doesn't always win the race, and the strongest warrior doesn't always win the battle. The wise sometimes go hungry, and the skilful are not necessarily wealthy. And those who are educated don't always lead successful lives. It is all decided by chance, by being in the right place at the right time* (Ecclesiastes 9:11, NLT).

Over the last decade or so I have enjoyed watching multiple gold-winning Olympic distance runner Mo Farah. He is an incredible athlete, and in recent years other athletes have tried every technique and strategy to beat him. One is to try running faster and getting out in front, gaining such a big lead that Mo cannot catch up. None of these strategies have worked as the fastest runner doesn't always win the race. Let's learn to slow down and make the right decisions.

Why are we in such a rush?
I suspect that we are victims of our instant and impatient age. I've lost count of the number of times I have counselled members of my congregation to slow down and take their time over a major decision. This has particularly been the case when a couple has decided to get married.

Life-defining decisions need time for prayerful consideration, and we must remember that God is rarely in the rush we are in. Neither is He slow in coming forward when He decides to speak into our plans and ideas. Our objective must be to avoid running ahead of Him or lagging behind. It's better to sleep on what you plan to do than to be kept awake by what you've done. It's so important that we take our time and seek God.

What are you living with now that you rushed into yesterday? Do you find yourself saying, "I wish I'd never..." or "If only I'd...."? Maybe you have trusted someone who wasn't worthy of your trust. Thank God that He is the God who rescues, restores and rebuilds broken lives. It's never too late to ask God to help you get your life back on track. While we may have to live with the consequences of our choices, God is faithful. He is more than capable of helping us create a new pathway to navigate through them. I've also discovered that, on occasions, God purposely allows me to suffer the consequences of my own actions for a period of time because He wants me to learn never to make that same mistake again. I guess that, like any good Father, He wants me to learn from my mistakes.

What are your children seeing?
When it comes to acknowledging God, let's make sure that we show our children what we're doing. They need to see us acknowledging Him._What are they seeing right now? Unless we want our children to ride on the back of our faith and never develop their own, we must

demonstrate our trust in God. Remember the exhortations in Deuteronomy 6:4-9 to talk about God in our homes. Our testimony is critical. Without it, our children will simply borrow our faith and never learn to depend on Him for themselves.

Seek His will in all you do

"Seek his will in all you do, and he will show you which path to take. Don't be impressed with your own wisdom. Instead, fear the Lord and turn away from evil" (Proverbs 3:6-7, NLT).

"Seek his will in all you do" is probably my favourite translation of all. He is omniscient; He knows all things. We must learn to seek His thoughts, which are always fully informed; His ways, which are always better ways than our ways. It's critical we discover what He thinks rather than making decisions based on what we or others think.

We have already noted that we must take care with our decisions. That means no rushing, no reacting, no hunches or gut feelings, but rather praying, seeking, doing the peace test and seeking the wise counsel of others.

David enquired of the Lord

The Old Testament records that King David specifically "enquired of the Lord" at least eight times during his leadership of Israel (for example in 1 Samuel 30:8 and 2 Samuel 5:19). There are countless other occasions when he sought God, but the Bible records that particular phrase eight times. We must also learn to seek His will in all we do, and even more so when we're faced by Philistines!

A brief study of how David sought God reveals so much. He never presumed anything, but simply chose to seek Him. David also discovered that God doesn't always work the same way twice. He's God, and He does His own thing. David was a mighty and experienced warrior who knew how to win battles. He knew more war strategies than anyone else, but he didn't presume anything. Maybe that's why he was so successful.

Notice what David does in these two battles:

> When the Philistines heard that David had been anointed king over Israel, they went up in full force to search for him, but David heard about it and went down to the stronghold. Now the Philistines had come and spread out in the Valley of Rephaim; so David inquired of the Lord, 'Shall I go and attack the Philistines? Will you deliver them into my hands?'

> The Lord answered him, 'Go, for I will surely deliver the Philistines into your hands.' So David went to Baal Perazim, and there he defeated them. He said, 'As waters break out, the Lord has broken out against my enemies before me.' So that place was called Baal Perazim. The Philistines abandoned their idols there, and David and his men carried them off.

> Once more the Philistines came up and spread out in the Valley of Rephaim; so David enquired of the Lord, and he answered, 'Do not go straight up, but circle around behind them and attack them in front of the poplar trees. As soon as you hear the sound of marching in the tops of the poplar trees, move quickly, because that will mean the Lord has gone out in front of you to strike the Philistine army.' So David did as the Lord commanded him, and he struck down the Philistines all the way from Gibeon to Gezer" (2 Samuel 5:17-25).

He didn't lean on his understanding or previous experiences. He didn't presume based on what had worked the last time. He enquired of the Lord. We must learn to enquire of the Lord! If we do, the promise of God is this:

"Call to me and I will answer you and tell you great and unsearchable things you do not know" (Jeremiah 33:3).

I wonder what you are doing right now that isn't working or has failed to alter the challenging situation you're facing. *"Well,"* you say, *"last time I needed a job, relationship, money or a breakthrough I did so and so... That's what worked last time..."*

I'll let you into a secret. God has different strategies for different situations. He doesn't always work the same way twice. Think of it like this. Five plus four equals nine, but six plus three also equals nine. In mathematics, you can use a different calculation to gain the same result, and God uses different strategies to achieve His will.

Who would have thought of marching around the city of Jericho once every day for six days and seven times on seventh day, then blowing trumpets shouting to cause the wall to fall down? It's not exactly one of the best-known strategies for taking a city! Who would have thought that bathing in the dirty River Jordan would cause leprosy to disappear from Naaman's skin, or that rubbing spit into a blind man's eyes would return his sight?

God wants to be involved in all your ways. In everything you do – whether your car engine has blown, studying at college is becoming a challenge or you're considering a new relationship, marriage or change of career – God loves to be involved. Can I encourage you to stop shutting Him out and start beginning to involve Him? Can I encourage you to get to know Him and His ways?

Jesus promised that we would not be left as orphans. We have the precious Holy Spirit as our counsellor; the one Jesus promised would lead us into all truth. So why not let Him lead?

Submit to Him

"In all your ways submit to him, and he will make your paths straight" (Proverbs 3:6).

Once we've acknowledged and really sought Him, the final, and critical, aspect is to submit ourselves to His better understanding.

Gideon

If you were planning to go to war against a cruel, fearful army, how would you do it? Gideon had a plan. He gathered together an army of some thirty-two thousand soldiers from various tribes to fight the Midianites, Amalekites and other peoples. There were so many enemy soldiers that the valley looked as though it was *"thick as locusts"*. Their camels *"could no more be counted than the sand on the seashore"* (see Judges 7:12).

Gideon's plan was simple: to outnumber the opposition armies and completely wipe them all out. That makes sense, but God had a different plan. He basically said: "Have fewer men than the enemy and I'll wipe them all out myself. If you've read the narrative before, you will know that, at God's insistence, the thirty-two thousand became ten thousand and finally just three hundred men. The chosen three hundred routed all the enemy armies with trumpets, lamps, empty jars and a lot of help from God.

When Gideon heard the dream and its interpretation, he bowed down and worshipped. He returned to the camp of Israel and called out, 'Get up! The Lord has given the Midianite camp into your hands.' Dividing the three hundred men into three companies, he placed trumpets and empty jars in the hands of all of them, with torches inside.

'Watch me,' he told them. 'Follow my lead. When I get to the edge of the camp, do exactly as I do. When I and all who are with me blow our trumpets, then from all around the camp blow yours and shout, 'For the Lord and for Gideon.'

Gideon and the hundred men with him reached the edge of the camp at the beginning of the middle watch, just after they had changed the guard. They blew their trumpets and broke the jars that were in their hands. The three companies blew the trumpets and smashed the jars. Grasping the torches in their left hands and holding in their right hands the trumpets they were to blow, they shouted, 'A sword for the Lord and for Gideon!' While each man held his position around the camp, all the Midianites ran, crying out as they fled.

When the three hundred trumpets sounded, the Lord caused the men throughout the camp to turn on each other with their swords. The army fled to Beth Shittah toward Zererah as far as the border of Abel Meholah near Tabbath" (Judges 7:15-22).

I suspect Gideon would have preferred the safety of numbers, but God had a plan and Gideon willingly submitted. That day, an incredible victory was won against all the odds. Why? Because Gideon knew God, sought God, listened to God, was led by God, trusted God and submitted to God. What a blueprint for our lives!

American pastor and author, Warren Wiersbe says: *"The word translated 'trust' in [Proverbs 3] verse 5 means 'to lie helpless, facedown.' It pictures a servant waiting for the master's command in readiness to obey, or a defeated soldier yielding himself to the conquering general."*[xlviii]

Gideon initialled refused the challenge to take on the Midianites:

"'But Lord,' Gideon replied, 'how can I rescue Israel? My clan is the weakest in the whole tribe of Manasseh, and I am the least in my entire family!'" (Judges 6:15, NLT).

However, somebody needed to lead Israel at that time, and God, as He so often does, called the guy who felt he was the weakest on earth. This is God's way. He so often uses the foolish things to shame the wise (see 1 Corinthians 1:27). Thankfully for Israel, as helpless as he felt, Gideon put himself on the line, trusted God and submitted to Him. There are occasions in all our lives when we have to take that position, even if we feel helpless. Maybe God is challenging you to stand like Gideon and bring deliverance to a nation, city, community or individual.

Perfect submission

When I was first called to ministry, serving as an intern (long before the title existed), my pastor used to send me to speak at a weekly elderly ladies' group called Women's Bright Hour. In its heyday, this group would have been full of vibrant younger women, but they had all grown old and would sit in a small room in the church knitting and chatting. They generally didn't listen, and even talked over the young intern, who was young, naive and a tad nervous about public speaking!

The main topic of discussion centred around which fish they were going to buy from the local shop for lunch, often while I was praying! However, many of these ladies really loved Jesus, and they loved the classic hymn "Blessed Assurance". They sang it every week, and the words are still engrained in my memory; especially the latter two verses, which remind us that there is blessing, goodness and rest in submitting to God.

The devil will throw us all the negatives, but when we truly trust God and are willing to submit to Him, "all is at rest", as the hymn declares. Why fight God? It's far better to submit and be at rest. It took me many years to learn the value of this. God really knows best, so I encourage you to trust and submit to Him in all your ways. Let Him lead.

Trusting God means letting go of our own way of doing things. It means surrendering our will for His. It means acknowledging that He is the leader of our lives and, just as importantly, that we are not. This means obeying Him at times when it perhaps appears crazy or even nonsensical.

Thank God that Peter submitted to a heavenly vision (see Acts 10:9-20) and was willing to visit Cornelius' house. Thank God that Ananias was willing to go and lay hands on Saul, who was able to share His newfound faith among the Gentiles. These men were willing to hear from God, do things differently and share the gospel with the wider world.

Imagine

Imagine how your world could change if you were willing to acknowledge Him in all your ways.

Consider the areas of your life in which you presume that what worked before will work again today. I wonder what you are doing that isn't working. Choose to enquire of the Lord. How about talking to God and asking for some fresh revelation and insight (that's acknowledging Him in all your ways, by the way).   Imagine how you could change the world for others if you really knew God, sought God, listened to God, were led by God, and were willing to trust and submit to God. If we trust God like we never have before, we will live like we never have before!

Chapter 9

He will make your paths straight

"You provide a broad path for my feet, so that my ankles do not give way" (Psalm 18:36).

As I look back on my personal journey, I can see that God has been straightening out and directing my paths. It's quite clear that God's fingerprints have been all over my life. Forensics would confirm God has been present all the time. In fact, as I reflect, I would suggest that God has been orchestrating, directing and straightening out my paths since before I was born. I'm sure the same is true for you.

I was about five or six when my parents told me I was adopted. I can remember walking to school that day thinking that I was special because my parents had chosen me to be their son. As a baby available for adoption, I'm more than aware that I could have ended up absolutely anywhere; however, God placed me in a Christian family.

My parents faithfully attended the local church, and I grew up with a solid understanding of the Christian faith. I became a Christian at about four years old and grew in my faith over the following years. My adopted mother came from a strong family of faith, and I caught it. I was encouraged to read autobiographies of the likes of missionary to China, Hudson Taylor, and reading those stories inspired me to have faith for incredible things from God. I learned to expect great things from Him and attempt great things for Him!

When I was about sixteen, I received some information about my heritage from my adopted parents. I had always felt like there was something missing from my life. Like most adopted children, I wanted to know where I had come from and where my roots were. I discovered that my real mother was from the very town I lived in (Leicester) and that my father was from Omaha, Nebraska. He had been a US air force engineer in Leicestershire during the early sixties.

At the time, I was simply happy to rest in this knowledge and get on with my life.

Having married Julia and had our first daughter, I decided it was time that I found my biological mother, which we did in 1989. It was amazing meeting her for the first time and introducing her to our young family. We have kept in contact and continue to visit her as often as we can. She is a wonderful lady who has not experienced the easiest of lives.

It wasn't until 2001 that God clearly directed me to find my biological father. I had been thinking about it for some years and had a deep longing in my heart to find my dad. I was at a church in Toronto and booked myself in for a prophetic group at which three ladies I had never met before prophesied over me. Wow! They were so accurate in describing my life at that moment. I was doing fine until one of them mentioned the importance for me of knowing who my father was. Deep sobs and tears followed as God made it clear that this was also important to Him.

On my return home, I started searching. I knew his name and where he lived. Within a few weeks of searching the internet I had found him and was calling him on the phone. I was pretty sure I had the right man, but what do you say to a man you've never met and who lives thousands of miles away when he answers his phone? I simply said, "Were you at Bruntingthorpe airfield in Leicestershire in the early sixties?" He replied, "Yes." So I said, "I think I'm your son!" He was absolutely ecstatic and told me he had always felt there was someone out there, though he had been unaware that my mother was pregnant at the time.

I soon discovered a whole new family in the US that I had no idea existed. They are wonderful people, and when Julia and I visited the first time they threw the most fantastic party for us in Omaha. I felt like the returning prodigal son. They are very special to me.

While in Omaha, I discovered a lot about my new family. My great-grandparents are of Syrian descent, from a place called Beit Lahia. Further to this, I discovered that my ancestors had been immigrants and had come to the US through Ellis Island. While the current family name is Koory, the original name was Khouri. I was amazed to discover that not only does the family tree go right back to Solomon, but that in Syrian the name "khouri" means "priest"!

This information completely blew me away. To think that one of my early ancestors was a priest and that, here I am, hundreds of years later, serving God as a priest. I look forward to meeting that guy one day in heaven. God has had his fingerprints all over my family down the centuries. He is an amazing God!

As I look back on my life, there have been so many coincidences or 'God-incidences'. A series of 'coincidences' caused my wonderful adopted parents to meet at a Christian camp all those years ago. In the early years of my career I missed out on two promotions I should have received and ended up in a relative backwater. It was there that a wonderful Christian minister took me under his wing, nurtured me and gave me opportunities to minister. It was at his tiny church in the Fenlands (near Peterborough) that God called me into ministry.

When this happened, I arrived back at just the right time to meet my wife and soulmate, Julia, who had been recently widowed. When God clearly directed us to go to Bible college, all the Baptist colleges were full, so we chose Elim, which has been our home for the past twenty-five years.

There are so many stories I could tell as I look back at the times when I have tried to trust God with all my heart and He has, in response, straightened out and directed my paths. The reason there is now a Dream Centre in Newcastle comes down to the fact that God prepared my heart, graciously gave me a vision and called me to the church in Newcastle where the former pastor had received a vision for 'God's dream building'! If you have been trusting God, you may well see the same pattern emerging as you look back. We shouldn't be surprised by this as it's what He has promised:

"I instruct you in the way of wisdom and lead you along straight paths" (Proverbs 4:11).

If we live out this amazing promise by trusting God, He will honour His part of the agreement. Imagine what God could trust you with tomorrow if you really trusted Him more today!

Going deeper

When I was a boy we used to sing a chorus called "When the Road is Rough and Steep". I loved that song. We sang it boisterously, particularly enjoying the fact back then that we could loudly stamp our feet twice at the end of several verses. The words of this simple chorus have stuck with me throughout my adult life. If we will trust Him enough and keep our eyes fixed on Him, Jesus will keep us on the straight and narrow road of life. In fact, He promises that if we keep our side of the deal He will direct our paths.

What kind of paths are they?

Commentators have debated for years the true meaning of 'paths' in this verse. What does it actually mean? The word we translate as 'path' is 'ôrach': a well-trodden road (literally or figuratively). The primitive root word 'yâshar', which we translate as 'make straight' means "to be (causatively to make) straight, level and lawful, and figuratively to be right, pleasant and prosperous". It can also mean "to make a straight path such as one for a king; free of obstacles and level".

Right paths

There is a sense that as we trust God with our lives and fully depend on Him, He will guide and straighten out our lives. While God is more concerned about us living in the right way than our own personal destiny and fulfilment, there is also a suggestion that He desires to guide us throughout our lives to help us to stay on the right (and righteous) path.

"He refreshes and restores my soul (life); He leads me in the paths of righteousness for His name's sake" (Psalm 23:3, AMP).

As a teenager, I attended a boys' camp (back in the day when girls weren't allowed, much to our frustration as young men!), and at the evening meeting in the marquee I remember singing an old chorus based on these words:

"Lead me, Lord, in your righteousness because of my enemies — make your way straight before me" (Psalm 5:8).

That simple chorus has been a regular prayer throughout my life. In many respects, it's a statement of submission and surrender to God. However, it is also a request for God to lead me into right living. Didn't Jesus say something about the importance of seeking first His Kingdom and righteousness (see Matthew 6:33)? As we trust and allow Him to straighten out our paths, God also does a work to straighten us out.

Guided paths
My desire is to live uprightly before God, but my prayer is also a request for Him to guide me throughout my life. David prayed:

"Make me to know your ways, O Lord; teach me your paths...for you are the God of my salvation..." (Psalm 25:4-5, ESV).

God promised through Isaiah that:

"The Lord will guide you continually..." (Isaiah 58:11, NLT).

The more time we spend with God, developing our relationships with Him, the more we will be open to the promptings and leading of the Holy Spirit. God will speak to us if we will only take the time to listen. So much of our Christian life depends upon us being responsive to the promptings of the Holy Spirit. He promises to guide us continually in the major and minor decisions of our lives. Can I encourage you to connect with God on a much more regular basis, and at a deeper level? If you trust God and learn to hear His voice clearly, imagine what He might guide you into tomorrow. That's very exciting!

"This is what the Lord says—your Redeemer, the Holy One of Israel: 'I am the Lord your God, who teaches you what is good for you and leads you along the paths you should follow'" (Isaiah 48:17, NLT).

Prosperous paths

David declared that: *"You have crowned the year with Your bounty and Your paths drip with fatness"* (Psalm 65:11, NASB).

So many of us struggle with our weight and are embarrassed when we are carrying a few extra pounds, but in biblical times 'fatness' was a sign of prosperity and material success. That sounds good to me! In fact, when Moses sent the twelve men to spy out the promised land, he asked them to report back on whether it was 'lean or fat'. They returned to say that the land was flowing with milk and honey (see Numbers 13:26-27). The land God had promised was incredibly fruitful.

It seems clear to me that God longs for us to prosper and experience His abundance. However, this will rarely be the case unless we choose to surrender our lives to Him and walk along His paths. Only *His* paths drip with fatness. Staying close to Him every day and allowing Him to guide us continually is the key to experiencing His blessing.

The *New Living Translation* puts this slightly differently, suggesting that even during periods of difficulty and challenge, when the paths become difficult to follow, they will overflow with abundance:

"You crown the year with a bountiful harvest; even the hard pathways overflow with abundance."

I guess this is hard to imagine unless you've experienced it, but God still blesses us, and even the toughest periods of our lives can be incredibly fruitful times in many ways.

"But blessed is the one who trusts in the Lord, whose confidence is in him. They will be like a tree planted by the water that sends out its roots by the stream. It does not fear when heat comes; its leaves are always green. It has no worries in a year of drought and never fails to bear fruit" (Jeremiah 17:7-8).

Whatever season you find yourself in right now, be aware that even in a season of drought it is possible to bear fruit. As I look back at some of my most challenging seasons, I realise that, unbeknown to me, I was still bearing fruit. I just didn't see it because at those times I was too concerned with merely surviving and getting through.

Clear and level paths

As we trust God and follow Him, He will straighten our paths and clear away or help us deal with any obstructions. *The New Bible Commentary* informs us that:

"To direct thy paths is to make the ways straight or plain, clearing obstructions. The word is used in Isaiah xl. 3 of clearing the highway in the desert."[xlix]

Isaiah declares:

Listen! It's the voice of someone shouting, 'Clear the way through the wilderness for the Lord! Make a straight highway through the wasteland for our God! Fill in the valleys, and level the mountains and hills. Straighten the curves, and smooth out the rough places. Then the glory of the Lord will be revealed, and all people will see it together. The Lord has spoken!' (Isaiah 40:3-5, NLT).

A public footpath in the countryside may be straight, but it is likely to be uneven and slippery, and there may be obstacles to navigate, such as rocks and stones, puddles, moss, nettles, tree roots and low-hanging branches. God promises that when we trust and acknowledge Him, He will make our paths level, firm and clear, but He didn't say that it would be easy, without any uphill climbs or obstacles. In fact, you may feel that because you're on a far-from-easy path, it isn't the right one. However, the difficult, tiring, uphill path can still be the right one. Think of Jesus going to the cross! (We'll cover that in more depth in the next chapter.)

God will clear some of the obstacles

As Julia and I (and countless others) have discovered, God is great at clearing obstacles and levelling the path.

In the *Amplified Bible*, Proverbs 3:6 says:

"In all your ways know and acknowledge and recognize Him, And He will make your paths straight and smooth [removing obstacles that block your way]."

In the CEV, it says:

"Always let him lead you, and he will clear the road for you to follow."

When we relocated to Newcastle to lead the church here in 2008, I accepted the position right at the end of May. In Britain, you have to apply for school places the previous autumn, and places are allocated during the winter. We started looking at schools for our daughter Amy in the middle of June, just a month before they closed for the summer holidays. There was little chance of getting a place for Amy at a good school, or so you might think. However, God miraculously cleared the way and she was offered places at two of the top schools in the city, both of which were oversubscribed at the time. God cleared the path for Amy to attend one of the best schools and her grades improved massively as a result. She is a teacher herself now.

"I will raise up Cyrus in my righteousness: I will make all his ways straight. He will rebuild my city and set my exiles free, but not for a price or reward, says the Lord Almighty" (Isaiah 45:13).

When we purchased the Dream Centre a few years later, we had to overcome all kinds of different obstacles and opposition (that's a story for another time), and God completely cleared the way, making straight paths for our feet. Every single obstacle was removed.

I'm convinced that there will be obstacles along the way, even if we're on the right path. They may come in the form of:

- Opposition, criticism and attacks (sometimes from family members and close friends)
- Doubts, anxieties and fears
- Negative voices

- Individual spiritual attacks, including sickness and other health issues
- A lack of resources and people
- Things getting worse before they get better

Having said that, God promises to either remove these obstacles or help us face them. I'm convinced that He allows many of them to develop our character, teach us, train us and refine us. He has certainly done this in my life, and I hope that I'm a better person and leader because of those obstacles.

One of the things Newcastle is known for is the fog on the River Tyne, so much so that a song has been written about it. There have been times when it's seemed as though there was a dense fog across the path I have been walking along with God. But rest assured that He sees the pathway even if all we can see is fog. God clears the fog and brings clarity of vision, enabling us to run with perseverance the race marked out for us.

God may have promised straight paths, but he never promised an easy journey or one without challenges. Sadly, some believers have been deceived into believing that the Christian life is one of constant victory and success, full of wealth, happiness and personal pleasure. The reality, as most of us have realised, is somewhat different. Nevertheless, the God in whom we trust has promised to be with us every step of the way.

"Trust in the Lord for ever, for the Lord, the Lord himself, is the Rock eternal...The path of the righteous is level; you, the Upright One, make the way of the righteous smooth. Yes, Lord, walking in the way of your laws, we wait for you; your name and renown are the desire of our hearts" (Isaiah 26:4:7-8).

Imagine

There is a wonderful promise for us if we follow the initial clauses of trusting with all our heart, not leading on our own understanding and acknowledging Him in all our ways. He will make our paths straight! Imagine what your life would be like if you lived out this incredible promise.

Maybe this is a moment to pause and reflect on the message of the book. Have you started to trust God more? Are you on the right path or is it time to get back on track? Please don't feel despondent if you've lost your way or been side-tracked. The devil's chief aim is to get us off course and separate us from God. Talk to Him now and get back on track. Ask Him to help you live out this great promise for the rest of your days.

Maybe this is the moment to claim this promise. You've been trusting Him, living right, letting Him lead and yet there are obstacles along the path you know He has placed you on. Don't be passive. Start to ask, seek, knock, petition, pray, contend and wrestle in prayer for this promise and watch God remove all the obstacles. He will do this; it's a promise!

Chapter 10

Discovering the right path

You're blessed when you stay on course, walking steadily on the road revealed by God. You're blessed when you follow his directions, doing your best to find him. That's right—you don't go off on your own; you walk straight along the road he set. You, God, prescribed the right way to live; now you expect us to live it. Oh, that my steps might be steady, keeping to the course you set; Then I'd never have any regrets in comparing my life with your counsel. I thank you for speaking straight from your heart; I learn the pattern of your righteous ways. I'm going to do what you tell me to do; don't ever walk off and leave me (Psalm 119:1-8, MSG).

As a boy, I must have walked up and down Snowdon, the highest mountain in Wales, half a dozen times. On the way down, we always descended by what was called the Pyg Track, one of the most popular but more rugged descents from the top of the mountain to the lakes. The descent is extremely steep as the track zigzags through the many old, redundant slate mines. It was anything but a straight path, and it took careful navigation.

Thank God that we had a very experienced group leader who had been up and down Snowdon numerous times and was able to direct us along the right path, which, while being the most direct route down the side of the mountain, was also a safe path. I doubt very much that we would have discovered it without his guidance.

The promise of God is this: if you will really learn to trust Him in every circumstance, if you depend on His understanding and not your own, then He will truly help you hit the right path and straighten it out for you.

Have you ever been on the wrong path?
"...He guides me along right paths, bringing honour to his name" *(*Psalms 23:3, NLT).

While we were recently on holiday in Wales, the man who owned the secluded cottage we stayed in told us there was a pathway down to a lovely bench overlooking the sea where we could watch the sun go down. He said it was a beautifully romantic spot. I'm all for a bit of holiday romance, so on the first evening we wandered off down the path only to end up in a massive field. I walked all around the field and along the cliffs but couldn't find the bench or the path that led to it. Eventually, we retraced our steps and found the right path, and yes, we had a romantic moment (I even received a peck on the cheek!) as the sun went down beyond the Irish Sea.

It's so easy to find ourselves on the wrong path. Media reports claimed that it was during a walking holiday that the British Prime Minister, Teresa May, decided to call a general election to increase her majority in the House of Commons. Many have suggested that she took a wrong path, and the election result backed this up (she lost her majority and had to form a coalition government). What looked like an appealing path turned out to be a disaster for her, the Conservatives and the nation. The Brexit negotiations then commenced, led by a government with a weakened mandate and low morale.

I've had friends in ministry who have moved to different churches with better facilities, a larger congregation and an improved salary, but have later discovered that, while the grass elsewhere appeared greener, it still needed cutting! There is a lesson there for all of us. It's critical that we find the right path and stay on it. The enemy will sometimes come disguised as an angel of light to tempt us away from the path God has placed us on with something that looks better. We must take care to refuse his advances.

It's so easy to get on the wrong path
The right path isn't necessarily the obvious one. The wrong path can also look like the right one at times.

"Enter by the narrow gate; for wide is the gate and broad is the way that leads to destruction, and there are many who go in by it. Because narrow is the gate and difficult is the way which leads to life, and there are few who find it" (Matthew 7:13-14, NKJV).

Following Jesus is not the easy option. It often means following the narrow, less attractive path. In *The Pilgrim's Progress*, Christian finds himself on the wrong path, having been advised by Mr Worldly Wiseman that it would be foolish of him to continue his pilgrimage, the end of which could only be hunger, pain and death. He told Christian it would be far better to settle down in the village of Morality, which would be a good place to raise a family because it was cheap to live there and they would have honest, well-behaved neighbours; people who lived according to the Ten Commandments.

It all looked and sounded good, but it was the wrong path. The right path will often, if not always, involve self-denial, surrender, submission, sacrifice and obedience as we take up our crosses daily. At times, it will mean saying no to things that appear attractive and easy, and saying yes to Kingdom matters.

There have been times in my life when I have become aware that I was on the wrong path. In some respects, it's easier to get back on the right path in the early days, but the longer you stay on the wrong path the tougher it becomes to leave it. And when you do, it can take a long time to rediscover the right path. If you find yourself on the wrong path, can I encourage you to get back on the right path, especially if the wrong one is sinful and could lead to entanglement? It's never too late. The writer to the Hebrews encourages us to cast off the sin that so easily entangles us (see Hebrews 12:1). Do it today!

Are you following two paths?
It's no more possible to follow two paths than it is to chase two bunnies. You will never catch them both. If you try to walk down two paths at the same time you will end up doing the splits (try it sometime!). You cannot walk down the worldly, sinful path and the Kingdom path at same time. You can try, but sadly the result will be pain and unhappiness.

"Come close to God, and God will come close to you. Wash your hands, you sinners; purify your hearts, for your loyalty is divided between God and the world" (James 4:8, NLT).

We follow two paths when:

- One moment we're blessing and the next we're cursing
- We sing about purity, then go home and view things we know we shouldn't
- Our Sunday standards and behaviours revert back on Monday morning
- We claim to trust God but try sort things out ourselves

"For your ways are in full view of the Lord, and he examines all your paths" (Proverbs 5:21).

Are you doing the splits? Do you have a foot on each path? What are you going to do about it? From personal experience, trying to keep a foot on each path is the most soul-destroying place to be. There is no peace and no happiness. Choose whom you will serve today.

Take the God path!
Jesus warned that the world offers many attractions. But as God's people we should always aim to take the narrow path. In spite of the enormous pressure from the world and its people, let's choose to trust and follow Him, for He knows best. He can only straighten out our paths if we're walking down the right ones. He promises to lead us along straight paths if we will let Him. Determine to stay away from every wrong path. In fact, as we read earlier, we should make a decision to "hate every wrong path" (see Psalm 119:104).

Sometimes even a good path isn't the best one. We want God's best! Proverbs says this not once, but twice:

"There is a way that appears to be right, but in the end it leads to death" (Proverbs 14:12; 16:25).

So please don't settle for:

- Cold, hard religion when you can have real faith and abundant living in Christ
- A second-rate job when you were created for better
- A boyfriend or girlfriend who is not God's best for you
- Friends who constantly let you down
- Any path that you know in your heart is wrong

You should never settle for second best, especially when a little bit of patience and persistence will pay great dividends. You only get one chance at this life!

How do we discover the right path?
"Let those who are wise understand these things. Let those with discernment listen carefully. The paths of the Lord are true and right, and righteous people live by walking in them. But in those paths sinners stumble and fall" (Hosea 14:9, NLT).

I love this verse, which talks so much about discerning the best path: the one that is true and right. Jesus, who declared Himself to be *"the way, the truth and the life"* (see John 14:6), promised before He went to the cross, that He would leave the Holy Spirit, whose chief role would be to guide us into all truth (see John 16:13). We can ask the Holy Spirit to be our guide and trust Him to lead us onto the right paths for our lives.

In many respects, I believe there are two clear paths for us to follow. There is a path we all follow as we pursue Christ. At this basic level, we live our lives as Christians adopting the basic disciplines and characteristics of the Christian faith, such as holiness, obedience, prayer, worship, service, evangelism and giving.

But there is another, more specific path that we should be following; one that applies to us as individuals. Each one of us is on a unique spiritual journey, created specifically for us. There were about thirty of us in my class at Bible college, and since graduation we have all followed different and unique paths, guided by the Holy Spirit. I believe the key to living life to the full is to follow Christ in whatever direction He leads. The writer to the Hebrews charged the believers to run the race marked out for them (see Hebrews 12:1), and this challenge still applies to us as individuals today.

Julia and I got married in 1987. I had already been called to full-time ministry and had been offered a place to train as a pastor at Spurgeon's College in London. However, as I mentioned earlier, their wise counsel was to delay my training for a couple of years in order to allow our marriage to settle.

This season came towards an end in early 1992 when God started to stir us and redirect our lives. He spoke to us in separate meetings on the same day in January, making it absolutely clear that He wanted us to go to Bible college that September. There were no places for several years at the Baptist training colleges, so we started to seek God concerning where I should train for ministry. A friend gave us this verse:

"This is what the Lord says: 'Stand at the crossroads and look; ask for the ancient paths, ask where the good way is, and walk in it, and you will find rest for your souls. But you said, "We will not walk in it"'" (Jeremiah 6:16).

We started to really seek God until He spoke to us, and it was my mother who suggested Elim Bible college (I have to admit that I had never heard of Elim!). We pushed at that door to see if it would open, and a few months later I started my ministry training. We love our Baptist foundation, but also enjoy being part of the wonderful Elim family. God clearly directed our path.

"Direct me in the path of your commands, for there I find delight" (Psalm 119:35).

It has been the same with every major decision. We have sought God and trusted Him to direct our paths as much as we were able, for walking under His direction is a delight.

How do we know we are on the right path?

Let's briefly return to that romantic walk towards the sea in Wales. We eventually discovered the right path to the beach, and as we retraced our steps that evening we realised there had actually been little pointers along the way. We perhaps should have realised that the little stream running alongside the path was heading for the sea. Then there was the increasing smell and sound of the sea that grew ever closer. But the biggest clue was a helpful little sign, previously unnoticed by us, which had an arrow that said 'BEACH' on it!

It's important to know that we're on the right path, and there will be confirmations along the way. God will signpost it in different ways. I mentioned in the previous chapter that we may experience lack, opposition and attack when we're on the right path. Rarely in my experience has everything gone smoothly and to plan. Despite this, there will be signs along the way to show us that we're going in the right direction.

I'll never forget my preparations for an important church meeting during the spring of 2014, prior to our purchase of the Dream Centre. I was concerned about ensuring that everyone was on board and felt directed by God to read through some of my predecessor's annual vision reports. I was amazed to read of a dream he had recorded in 2006, which, until that moment, I had been completely unaware of:

On the Saturday evening before my very first Sunday, I prayed over the building, standing on the platform. I prayed quoting Isaiah 54:2-3 that we would overflow into the foyer, so much so that we would need a new building.

He went on to share his dream for the next three to five years:

I felt the Spirit say that the enlargement that we will experience will be bigger than anything I could imagine. The work would be big, strategic in the city; everyone will look at it and marvel at the wonder of God. That something of our vital worship and work of God would go around the world. Some people might say 'I wonder whether the pastor suffers from delusions.' My reply is: 'This is my dream of God.' Joseph dreamed a big dream many centuries ago. He was misunderstood, ridiculed and opposed. He experienced a number of setbacks, reaching an all-time low in prison. The dream of God within him enlarged his capacity to trust in God and declare his tomorrow.

He went on to add (under the heading "New Dream Building"):

We have been looking at our facilities for the last few years. We are aware that we have well and truly outstripped our present building and need something much larger. My ultimate dream for our new building is for a 700-seater auditorium, conference/worship centre, with an elegant cafe bar and cutting-edge resource centre. I dream that it will have first class vision and sound, and ample rooms and facilities that will prove to be a Christian life centre for our city and beyond.

It was an incredible feeling to realise that what Adrian Mancini had foreseen in the Spirit was coming to fruition. Of course, I should not have been surprised by this. God expects us to take prayerfully considered steps of faith and will often confirm His will once you're on the move (see Isaiah 30:21). God doesn't send confirmations of directions to stationary people, and as we discovered earlier He promises to make the paths we take straight.

The journey may well be full of obstacles and seemingly insurmountable challenges to begin with, but God will deal with them one by one. The Christian walk is a journey of faith and personal growth. If there were no obstacles or challenges, we would remain weak and feeble in our faith. God wants people who are strong, faith-filled and who trust Him enough to achieve great exploits for Him.

Sometimes the right path is a completely new path

God gave me fresh revelation of this as I spent a day praying and seeking Him at a beautiful Anglican retreat in the wonderful Northumberland countryside. At the time, our church was preparing to relocate from the old congregational building to the Dream Centre.

I had spent the day seeking God and fasting, and in the early afternoon I went for a walk along the dene where the river runs. I often find that God speaks through what I see. As I walked along the top of the gorge looking down on the river below, I discovered a new path. I followed it all the way along, and as I walked I noticed waterfalls I had never seen before. As I continued, I noticed that where the lower path meandered alongside the river, the ground had been cleared. Trees had been cut down, foliage had been uprooted and new saplings had been planted to make way for a further path.

As I walked and prayed, I asked God whether He was trying to say anything to me. Nothing came immediately. As I moved further along, I noticed some sheep peering at me through the fence and wondered if they had any great insights, but sadly they had nothing to say! I have learned to wait on God and be patient as I listen for Him to speak.

I looked across the gorge and the sun broke through the clouds for the first time that day. Immediately, God said to me, "A new day has dawned." I replied, "It's two fifty pm!" God then told me the following (which is combination of Ecclesiastes 3:2, Isaiah 43:19 and 2 Cor. 5:17):

"See, I am doing a new thing! The old has gone, the new day has come. It's time to uproot and plant, and time to take a new path. A new day requires a new path!"

It's interesting that God never says: "See, I am doing an old thing", and He rarely says, "I want you to go down an old path." He is the God who makes all things new. Maybe you are standing on the brink of something new right now. Have you perceived it yet? Maybe it's a new day. There is a new path for the new day! Maybe it's time to reflect, uproot and plant. And maybe things will never be the same.

Consider the following questions:

- What new path is God asking you to walk down?
- What new adventure does He have for you?
- What is He asking you to uproot and plant?
- What might God trust you with tomorrow if you learned to trust Him more today?

As I stood and prayed at the spot in the photo, God showed me something else. There was another new path: it was lower down the gorge and it came to a dead end. He said this: "Simon, notice how I've brought you on the higher path."

He reminded me of Isaiah 55:8-9:

"'For my thoughts are not your thoughts, neither are your ways my ways,'" declares the Lord. "'As the heavens are higher than the earth, so are my ways higher than your ways and my thoughts than your thoughts.'"

Or, as *The Message* says: *"I don't think the way you think. The way you work isn't the way I work."*

Then He said: "This is a time to seek Me for My ways. My thoughts are higher than your thoughts could ever be. You have limited sight." Regarding the lower path, which came to a dead end, I felt God say that some people have been on the same path for so long they haven't realised that it's a road to nowhere; that it's a dead-end street.

We must take care that we don't end up on that street, because it's a road to nowhere. Let's seek Him for His higher ways and deeper thoughts. Jesus said: *"My sheep listen to my voice!"* (See John 10:27). Stop fumbling around in the dark!

One of my favourite police dramas is called *Silent Witness*. It's about a team of forensic pathologists who attempt to solve murders, some of which are from many decades ago. In one episode, they were in a very dark building and were fumbling around trying to discover a clue. Everything within me wanted to shout at the TV: "Someone get a torch! Turn a light on!"

You probably know people who have spent their entire lives fumbling around in the dark. It would appear that they have wasted years of their lives without really going anywhere, never quite finding their niche, perhaps not yet having discovered the right career or life partner for them. It is so tragic to watch people waste the fleeting time they have in this world.

If that's you reading this book, I want to encourage you to seek God. He has an amazing plan and purpose for your life that only you can fulfil. You are the perfect person and the perfect fit for a life that only you can live, and once you discover and walk in it you will be incredibly fulfilled. There is no need to take any more 'wrong paths'. If you seek God and put Him first, He promises to guide you onto the right path and to make that path straight. Don't miss out for a second longer. And once you've found the right path, stay on it!

As a boy, I grew up watching the silky skills of one of the greatest footballers who ever lived. George Best was an incredible winger who terrorised defenders across Europe. He played for one of the greatest teams in the UK, Manchester United, and also for his country, Northern Ireland. His manager at Manchester United, Sir Matt Busby, described him as a genius.

Sadly, George failed to stay on the right path and retired suddenly at the age of twenty-seven. He admitted in later years that: "I spent a lot of money on booze, birds [women] and fast cars. The rest I squandered."[1] His life ended tragically aged fifty-nine due to complications while having a second liver transplant. George drank himself into an early grave. What a tragedy! It all started when he became side-tracked as a result of his fame and fortune. While this is an extreme example, it's a good reminder of the value of staying on the right path.

As we have already discussed, the path of life is a journey full of high and lows, ups and downs, successes and failures. Thank God that He promises to help us stay on track. However, He won't do it all for us. He expects us to play our part. This involves a fair bit of determination and personal discipline. It's not easy at times, and pastors and leaders face exactly the same challenges as anyone else.

Whatever our position in life, I believe the benefits of trusting God and staying on the right path far outweigh the disadvantages.

British author CS Lewis wrote: *"One road leads home and a thousand roads lead into the wilderness."*[li]

Imagine

It's so important that we discover the right path for our lives. We're all called to pursue Christ and to follow Him along the path of Christian growth and discipleship; however, there is a specific path that God has called each of us to follow.

I've known people who have attempted to follow the same paths as others, but that hasn't been the right path for them. This has led to frustration, restriction and disappointment. God has uniquely shaped each one of us for a unique path. People can join us for seasons on that path, or even for life if we get married. Let's be careful that we don't follow any paths that 'just seem right' because this can lead to 'death' (hopefully not physically!) in all kinds of ways. Let's choose to enter through the narrow gate and follow the path that leads to life in all its abundance.

If you haven't found that specific and unique path yet, why not pause and surrender your life to Christ right now and ask Him to help you discover the specific path for your life? Then continue to seek Him over the coming weeks. You may well be amazed at what He leads you into.

Part III

Everyday trust

"Anyone who trusts in me will not be disappointed"
(Isaiah 49:23, NCV)

Chapter 11

Through the dark and difficult days

'If you'll hold on to me for dear life,' says God, 'I'll get you out of any trouble. I'll give you the best of care if you'll only get to know and trust me. Call me and I'll answer, be at your side in bad times; I'll rescue you, then throw you a party. I'll give you a long life, give you a long drink of salvation!' (Psalm 91:14-16, MSG).

Dark days

I will never forget May 23rd, 2014, and the devastating phone call I received from my tearful and shocked daughter, Amy: "Sarah is dead! Sarah is dead!"

For a moment, my world collapsed at the thought that my own daughter, also called Sarah, had died. Somehow composing myself, I asked, "Sarah who?"

Amy's closest friend, Sarah Crooks, had just been found by her father, George, having passed away tragically in her sleep aged twenty-three. So commenced an incredibly dark period in that family's life, and in the lives of all those who knew and loved her. Sarah wasn't just an amazing daughter to George and Helen, but an incredible friend and very much loved by us all.

I will never forget the long lines of devastated people queuing for the funeral service of that wonderful young lady. Nor will I forget the months of depression so many people in our congregation experienced, including Amy. We watched our normally happy-go-lucky, faith-filled daughter struggle through the grief, loss and desperation of those months. There is nothing you can say that helps.

It was a dreadfully dark period for us, and we remained vigilant and very concerned for our daughter, but of course Sarah's family experienced even greater grief. I can't imagine what they suffered. I have to say that, though they remain devastated, their trust in God somehow got them through. They amaze me. I have no idea how I would have responded, but I hope I would have somehow trusted God.

Whether we like it or not, we will all face dark days. It might be the loss of a loved one, a life-threatening disease, redundancy, personal attacks, threats, bullying, loss or financial disaster. At times like this, we need to trust God more than ever before.

Dark seasons

I love the call of God on my life. I often tell people it's the best job in the world, especially when you see how He transforms people's lives, but at times it can sometimes feel like the worst job in the world. The pressures of local church leadership can be heavy and all-consuming at times.

I have experienced incredibly dark days, and sometimes these days become weeks, months and years. I know how it feels to be lied about, misrepresented, to have my character assassinated and to have people who were formerly friends cross the road so they didn't have to talk to me. I have received threats and been attacked verbally. I have even been wished dead by some on social media, and my character has been called into question in the press.

I have had people write horrible things about me that simply aren't true. On one occasion, a guy wrote to every member of my congregation and told lies about me. Julia really struggled for the best part of a year because of the haters, and my children also suffered badly.

I remember years ago standing in the office of my regional leader with tear-filled eyes offering to resign. My ministry nearly came to a premature end in those early years. Sadly, all these actions were perpetrated by God's own people. We have forgiven them and are keenly aware that we are far from perfect, and we certainly made mistakes during that period. In spite of these attacks, which will most likely affect anyone in Christian leadership, we have to be patient and trust God in these dark seasons, believing that better days lie ahead.

I'm sure you will have experienced similarly difficult circumstances, whether at home, in your family, at work or in church life. My heart goes out to all those who have suffered serious illnesses, the loss of precious loved ones and other difficult situations. These things really challenge our faith and trust in God.

A dark season of the soul

In 2016, I endured a horrendous and very distressing mental and physical battle. I can only say that it was an attack of the enemy. This is what I recorded in my journal during June:

My life has become such a battle field right now. The enemy seems to be coming in like a flood attacking my health, strength and energy and making me believe his lies. I have to daily, almost hourly, resist him until he flees from me. I declare that no weapon formed against me will prosper and also that, YES! I refute & silence (!) every lie spoken against me (not just by humans but by the enemy against and to me!).

During this dark season, which initially lasted for about eight months, my mind was constantly full of horrific thoughts and speculations. I couldn't sleep at night as I would start shaking and having cold sweats. During the day I was experiencing body tremors, shaking, slurring, twitching, and pins and needles in my arms. I didn't know whether I was having a breakdown or not, but I became absolutely convinced that there was something seriously wrong with me, and that I had a life-changing illness.

In my sleep I heard the devil say of something I was dreaming about: "You'll be dead by the time that happens." I couldn't concentrate, and I became forgetful. I seemed to have some kind of memory fog. When I was talking to people I appeared to be present, but my mind was a million miles away with thoughts of death and horrific speculations.

The Bible suggests that there will be times when the enemy comes in like a flood, and that was certainly my experience:

"When the enemy comes in like a flood, The Spirit of the Lord will lift up a standard against him" (Isaiah 59:19).

Thankfully, God provided a way out for me via Kris Vallotton's brilliant book, *Spirit Wars*. That book really helped to set me free. Kris had been through a similar, but much worse, experience and found freedom and release in quoting the words of Paul in 2 Timothy 1:7:

"For God has not given us a spirit of fear, but of power and of love and of a sound mind."

We are in a real battle as God's people. During and following that dark season of the soul, I had to learn to trust God again on a daily basis. The attacks didn't stop immediately, and I had some setbacks, but He taught me how to fight and has brought me through. Praise God! When I felt weak and weary from fighting the enemy I had to allow the Lord to raise His royal ensign (banner), proclaiming who He was and what He stands for so that the enemy would flee. This meant trusting Him to act on my behalf during some very dark days.

I also had to learn to resist the devil myself until he left me alone. One of my common prayers was this: "Father, I don't just want to be strong in the Lord and in His mighty power [see Ephesians 6:10], I want to have a strong mind so I can resist the enemy's attacks." Like David, I've learned that:

"He trains my hands for battle; my arms can bend a bow of bronze" (Psalm 18:34).

Trusting God when everything goes pear-shaped

I'm sure most of us have experienced seasons when if anything could go wrong it did. How come the washing machine breaks down at the exact same time the car needs a new tyre and the rent goes up? Sometimes it feels like there's more month than money, and it can become a whole lot worse than that.

When troubles come, do you still trust God? When the muck hits the fan, do you have faith in Him? Sometimes, as my godly mother used to say, you have to choose to trust, and cling on by your fingernails if needs be. But if you can somehow cling to Him, God will prove Himself faithful.

When the going gets tough, the tough get going!

Billy Ocean's hit record reminds us how important it is to respond well (with a bit of fight!) during dark seasons. So how do we trust God during our darkest days? How do we respond when our circumstances are tough?

There are some obvious things we can do, such as staying close to our Father God in prayer and pouring out our hearts to Him in worship. I've discovered some other helpful ways of walking in faith through the hardest seasons.

Don't dwell in the dark place

Stop thinking and talking about your difficult situation all the time. This will make you feel even worse and bring everyone around you down. I had to learn this lesson myself. We are responsible for the spiritual atmosphere in our homes and in our relationships. Pity parties help no one, least of all the ones going through tough times.

One way we can help ourselves is to take an interest in someone else who is going through a dark season, doing our best to support and encourage them. I've found this a helpful way to take the focus off my own problems. The plus side is that we always feel better when we're helping others.

Remember what God has done in the past

I have found this particularly helpful during the darkest of times. I try to recall all the occasions in the past when God has helped, rescued, answered prayer, provided for, delivered and surprised me. I then ask myself the question: "After God has done all that, is He about to let me down now?"

When I'm struggling with my calling and the challenges of leading our church, and self-doubt begins to creep in, I remind myself that God has gone to a lot of trouble to get me this far, and that He's very unlikely to let me down now. He has invested too much in me, and besides, He is a good God. As I do these things, I feel like I'm resetting my hard drive so I can go out and face the world again.

Seek support and encouragement from others

No man (or woman) is an island. We need the love, support, comfort and encouragement of other people. This is one of the reasons why small groups are so important in church life. I discovered the value of being able to support individuals through the dark days during my time as a small group leader. I encouraged our group to pray people through their difficulties. We would pray for them when we met as a group, but we also committed to pray for individuals every day until something changed. We saw so many miracles and answers to prayer. If you're experiencing a dark season, seek the support and encouragement of others. You won't regret it.

Stand on the promises of God

Paul taught the Corinthian believers that: *"...All of God's promises have been fulfilled in Christ with a resounding 'Yes!'"* (see 2 Corinthians 1:20, NLT). The very next verse promises that: *"It is God who enables us, along with you, to stand firm for Christ..."*

During the darkest of times, we must stand on God's promises. Peter shares that:

"His divine power has given us everything we need for a godly life through our knowledge of him who called us by his own glory and goodness. Through these he has given us his very great and precious promises, so that through them you may participate in the divine nature, having escaped the corruption in the world caused by evil desires" (2 Peter 1:3-4).

There is a sense in which God enables us to stand firm in Christ during particularly dark seasons. Don't forget to stand on the things God has already promised you and prophesied over your life. What has He already said? What has He already promised to do? Stand on it. Speak it out. Declare it!

The longer it lasts, the closer you are to the end

One of things I have discovered during the longest hard seasons is that I have found it easy to believe that it will last forever. However, this is misleading, because often the longer it goes on the closer you are to a breakthrough or a solution. Darkness turns to light in a split second. The flick of a switch can change everything in a moment.

English theologian, Thomas Fuller, is quoted as saying: *"It is always darkest just before the day dawneth."*[lii]

As I write this, I'm praying for those of you who are experiencing deep darkness that dawn will swiftly come, and with it the morning chorus of praise songs, a fresh dew (God's favour and anointing) and new beginnings. He is the God who makes all things new.

Recognising God's pruning

"I am the true grapevine, and my Father is the gardener. He cuts off every branch of mine that doesn't produce fruit, and he prunes the branches that do bear fruit so they will produce even more" (John 15:1-2, NLT).

Pruning can be a painful experience. God prunes for two reasons, and we often forget the second one. Primarily, a gardener will prune anything that *isn't* fruitful. That makes sense. Secondly, a gardener will prune what *is* fruitful. Even a well cultivated plant will only produce limited fruit if left to its own devices. Pruning is the process wherein the gardener cuts back part of the plant, sometimes quite severely, in order to allow the plant to focus its nutrients in fewer places, resulting in a more fruitful plant.

This can be hard for us to bear. There have been times in my ministry when God has pruned me in both areas, and the second type of pruning can be hard to accept.

Several years ago, I stood down as leader of a Christian summer camp. I had been involved in attending and serving at camps since I was seven years old. During the latter ten years I had been leading them. Stepping down was an incredibly painful experience for me, and it carried a great sense of loss and bereavement. I stopped attending summer camps altogether. I love these events, and the whole community vibe and camaraderie. I eventually came to terms with this and trusted God that some pruning was occurring, but it was still incredibly hard.

When our Father the gardener gets those shears out, we must simply trust Him, allowing Him to do what's best and embracing the changes He is bringing to pass. He is, after all, a very experienced gardener, and He does it so that our lives will become even more fruitful!

Since I stepped down from the camp, I have found more time for blogging and writing. This book has come about as a result of that, and in recent months an exciting additional ministry opportunity that precisely fits who I am and who God has called me to be has opened up. It appears God knew what He was doing! He is after all, the Alpha and the Omega. God knows the end from the beginning, and He knew what He was going to open up for me if I simply trusted Him during the difficult pruning season.

Trusting God isn't always easy. It means embracing change, and that can be challenging and even scary at times. I've had moments of sheer desperation and anxiety on occasion. God will occasionally take us to the edge, but one thing I've learned is this: He is Faithful and will never ever break His promises. To do so would mean that He wasn't actually God, as God never denies His own Word.

Jesus trusted and followed God right through to the cross. It wasn't easy for Him, and there are times when it won't be easy for us. But never forget that after the cross came resurrection! We are called to take up our cross and follow Him each day. That's the cost of trusting God with all our heart.

Encourage yourself in the Lord
I love the story in 1 Samuel 30 where David has returned to Ziklag to discover that the Amalekites have raided his camp. By the time David and his men entered the village, it had been burned to the ground, and the men's wives, sons, and daughters had been taken prisoner. The Bible records that David and his men burst out in loud wails and wept until they were exhausted with weeping. Their distress soon turned to anger and bitterness, and the men even began to talk of stoning David. I don't think things could have been much darker for David at that moment.

What would you have done in those circumstances? David's response is a lesson for us all:

"David strengthened himself with trust in his God. He ordered Abiathar the priest, son of Ahimelech, 'Bring me the Ephod so I can consult God.' Abiathar brought it to David" (1 Samuel 30:6-7, MSG).

We know from the narrative that God guided David (with the Ephod) to go after the band of raiders, and everyone and everything was rescued and recovered. In fact, God blessed David with an additional hoard of plunder that day. We can only speculate as to what happened to David in that moment. I suspect that in the midst of the crisis and the threat to His life, David threw himself on God, and God ministered to him in a unique way.

I imagine He reminded David of all the times in the past that He had rescued and provided for him. He probably said to David: "You trusted me with the lion and the bear as a young shepherd. As a teenage boy I was there as you faced Goliath. I've rescued you from the Philistines and from the hand of Saul. I sent Samuel to choose you from all your brothers to be the next king of Israel. Do you really think I've brought you this far to let you down now?"

During a particularly difficult time in the last few years, I was having a similar conversation with God while on a long walk with Alfie, my little black dog. He must be the most sanctified dog in the world as he listens to a lot of my prayers and conversations with God. Every pastor should have one! On this particular night, I was pouring my heart out to God and sharing my doubts and fears. My Father God gently encouraged me and asked me to stop talking as He had something to say. This is what he shared with me that night:

I redeemed your life from the pit. I rescued you when there was no one else to do so. You are My precious child. Do you really think I would forget you now? I will never leave you or forsake you. I am your redeemer, rescuer and strong tower. I will fully restore you, and you will have no fear of bad news, for I am your God. Yes, Satan has asked to sift you like wheat, but I am praying for you, Simon, that your faith will not fail. When you come through this, strengthen your brothers.

I cannot express how deeply those simple words encouraged and strengthened me that night, and I have stood on them several times since. In the darkest of moments, it's good to know that we have a Father who cares, and who is only too ready to strengthen us and rebuild our trust in Him.

Imagine if David hadn't trusted God at that moment. Imagine if he hadn't known what to do or whom to turn to. Imagine if he hadn't rallied the troops. He could have been killed by his own men and nothing would have been recovered. The additional plunder would have been lost, in addition to the loss of life and his kingship. When the dark days come, it's critical that we learn to really trust. If we trust God more today, imagine what He will trust us with and lead us into tomorrow!

American athlete Allyson Felix said: *"The most important lesson that I have learned is to trust God in every circumstance. Lots of times we go through different trials and following God's plan seems like it doesn't make any sense at all. God is always in control and he will never leave us."*[liii]

Don't quit!

I have been tempted to quit many times. Like any calling in life, ministry certainly has its moments. Sometimes when we have stepped out in faith and made major decisions, challenges and obstacles arise. The enemy hates it when God's people trust Him. This often brings a retaliatory attack of some kind. However, if we really trust God we will refuse to quit.

Sir Winston Churchill was one of our greatest prime ministers. Many people credit Britain's Second World War victory to Churchill's tenacity, leadership and fearlessness in the face of a powerful German threat. What was it that inspired him to stand so steadfastly and inspire a nation to endure great hardships and to win against all the odds?

Perhaps his secret is found in an old story I read about him. In later life, Churchill was invited to speak at a British university. During the journey there, the car had a problem, which meant he arrived so late that there was no time left for a long speech. So instead, he was invited to say just a few words. In his gruff manner, he stood before the young graduates, paused and then boomed: "Never give up." He paused for about thirty seconds and then said: "Never, never, give up!" Finally, after a much longer pause, he declared: "Never, never, *never* give up!" He returned to his seat, and the audience gave him a standing ovation.[liv]

When writing about the importance of perseverance, Churchill wrote:

"Never give in, never give in, never, never, never, never - in nothing, great or small, large or petty - never give in except to convictions of honour and good sense."[lv]

The words "never give in" should be written on our hearts. Perseverance is one of the primary qualities that will enable us to stay on the right path and live effective, productive lives.

For this very reason, make every effort to add to your faith goodness; and to goodness, knowledge; and to knowledge, self-control; and to self-control, perseverance; and to perseverance, godliness; and to godliness, brotherly kindness; and to brotherly kindness, love. For if you possess these qualities in increasing measure, they will keep you from being ineffective and unproductive in your knowledge of our Lord Jesus Christ (2 Peter 1:5-8).

It may seem like an old-fashioned word, but the Bible has a lot to say about perseverance. It means standing firm under pressure. It means trusting God and not quitting despite what we see, even if it isn't what we initially anticipated after making a prayed-through, God-guided, major decision. We must choose to stick with these decisions and not quit before we've given God time to bring about the anticipated results. During this waiting period, we must trust God emphatically.

In all this, I believe God will bless and sustain us during periods of prayed-through change. We cannot remain in the same position all our lives. Big decisions have to be made in order for us to experience all that God planned for us before we were even born. God blesses perseverance, and there will be rewards along the way in addition to the promise of the eternal reward.

"Blessed is the man who perseveres under trial, because when he has stood the test, he will receive the crown of life that God has promised to those who love him" (James 1:12, *Berean Study Bible*).

Real trust brings real benefits

When we really learn to trust God, the benefits are huge. Naturally, we rarely learn to trust Him during seasons of blessing and prosperity. In my experience, it's during the darkest seasons that we really learn to do so. In some respects, we have little choice. As I reflect on my life, I'm actually thankful for some of those dark days, as God has used what the enemy meant for harm to develop my character and faith. Trust brings the following things to the table during the difficult and dark days.

Security

We become more secure in God. I love the way *The Message* translates Psalm 23:4:

"Even when the way goes through Death Valley, I'm not afraid when you walk at my side. Your trusty shepherd's crook makes me feel secure" (Psalm 23:4, MSG).

When you know that God has carried you through difficult situations, it creates an incredible sense of security. I know now, from personal experience, that my God is faithful and will never let me down. My security and trust are in no one else. My confidence is in Him alone.

Assurance

There is great assurance in the knowledge that God is with us, and that He never slumbers or sleeps. He is often working behind the scenes on our behalf. For the most part, we remain oblivious to what He is doing until what I can only describe as a 'suddenly moment' occurs. When we believe that nothing is happening and are becoming frustrated at God's apparent lack of action, His silent action suddenly comes into public view and we are blown away. I love it when God does that. We must remain expectant that God is about to release a 'suddenly' into our situation.

Increased faith

I've seen buildings being constructed in other parts of the world and have shuddered. The foundations are so shallow and the support structures are poor. I wouldn't want to stay in one of those places! Trust is the foundation upon which our faith is built. As our trust grows, so does our faith. If we don't really trust God, we're unlikely to take faith steps, let alone achieve anything of eternal consequence. Besides that, it is impossible to please God without faith (see Hebrews 11:6).

Incredible peace

When we really trust God, we discover an incredible God-given sense of peace, even during the toughest of times. Constant worry creates anxiety, sleeplessness, lack of focus, sickness, memory loss and so on, but trusting God creates an oasis of calm in a turbulent sea.

"You will keep in perfect peace all who trust in you, all whose thoughts are fixed on you! Trust in the Lord always, for the Lord God is the eternal Rock" (Isaiah 26:3-4, NLT).

Paul talks about the incredible peace of God, which *"transcends all understanding"* and will *"guard [our] hearts and [our] minds in Christ Jesus"* (see Philippians 4:7). It's a perfect, undiluted, supernatural and unexplainable peace that I have experienced many times in my life when confronted by darkness, anxieties, worries and fears about my family and my health, and by threats from others. The peace God provides when we really trust Him is amazing. I cannot explain it, but God provides it and guards our minds with it. This incredible peace has been promised to each of us. Have you discovered it yet?

Joy

David, who trusted God emphatically, declared:

"The Lord is my strength and shield. I trust him with all my heart. He helps me, and my heart is filled with joy. I burst out in songs of thanksgiving" (Psalms 28:7, NLT).

"Oh, the joys of those who trust the Lord, who have no confidence in the proud or in those who worship idols" (Psalms 40:4, NLT).

The Apostle Peter, who experience all kinds of threats and persecution, was able to say:

"You love him even though you have never seen him. Though you do not see him now, you trust him; and you rejoice with a glorious, inexpressible joy. The reward for trusting him will be the salvation of your souls" (1 Peter 1:8-9, NLT).

It might seem impossible to experience any kind of joy during a difficult season; however, I have discovered that joy is available if we ask for it. The joy of the Lord is our strength (see Nehemiah 8:10), and we should seek it. God will fill our hearts with joy, and when that happens strength arises, our hearts are renewed, and we are able to live to fight another day.

"You have made known to me the paths of life; you will fill me with joy in your presence" (Acts 2:28).

Confidence in God

Real trust brings confidence in God. This is connected to our sense of security in Him. At moments when I have been at my lowest ebb, the Holy Spirit has stepped in and reminded me of all that God has done in the past. My confidence in God has then risen up again.

"I remain confident of this: I will see the goodness of the Lord in the land of the living. Wait for the Lord; be strong and take heart and wait for the Lord" (Psalm 27:13-14).

Even in the darkest times we must remain confident in God. Our enemy, the devil, will try to tell us the opposite and create all kinds of 'what if?' and worst-case scenarios in our heads, but we need to remain confident in our God.

Dutch Christian, Corrie ten Boom, who was imprisoned for hiding Jews from the Nazis said: *"When a train goes through a tunnel and it gets dark, you don't throw away the ticket and jump off. You sit still and trust the engineer."*[lvi]

Let's keep our confidence in the 'Engineer'. Let's choose to live by faith, not by sight (see 2 Corinthians 5:7).

Trusting builds faith

"Consider it pure joy, my brothers and sisters, whenever you face trials of many kinds, because you know that the testing of your faith produces perseverance. Let perseverance finish its work so that you may be mature and complete, not lacking anything" (James 1:2-4).

We must understand that dark days help us build faith in God.

Scottish philosopher, Thomas Carlyle, said: *"Adversity is the diamond dust Heaven polishes its jewels with."*[lvii]

Car manufacturers will often test a new car for days before deciding whether or not it is roadworthy and can be entrusted to the public. We are no different. God allows our faith to be tested at times, so that we will trust Him in all the future plans He has for us. Tough days and challenging seasons help us become more mature and complete. They are critical moments in God's personal development plan for our lives.

When we trust Him through trials, our faith increases and we experience increased security. His desire is that, in an increasingly insecure and unstable world, there is one place where we can safely place our trust: solely in Him. I'll say it once again: if we trust God like we never have before, we will live like we never have before.

Imagine

My heart goes out to you if you're experiencing one of those dark seasons right now. Maybe you're feeling deeply discouraged. Perhaps you are experiencing incredible pain, loss and despair, and you're probably wondering if it will ever end. Can I encourage you to pour your heart out to God? Find a quiet place where you can talk with your Father alone and tell Him exactly how you feel.

Ask Him to take away all the negative feelings and to replace them with His perfect peace, which passes all understanding. Ask Him to carry you through this season and give you the strength, faith and the trust you need for each day. Ask him to speak to you personally. Ask Him to fill your heart with His unexplainable joy and a renewed hope in Him: that the God who has brought you this far is not about to fail you in your darkest hour. Remember that He is faithful and worthy of your complete trust.

Chapter 12

When nothing appears to change

There was a man who became shipwrecked on a deserted island many years ago. He managed to build himself a hut to live in, using it to store the possessions he had salvaged from his boat. He would watch every day for signs of a ship or aeroplane passing by. He prayed to God for help. Some days, he became discouraged and wondered if he would ever get off that island, but still he prayed.

One day, he was over the other side of the island and noticed smoke rising from the direction of his hut. He ran back as quickly as he could, only to realise that his worst fears had come true. His hut and all his belongings had been destroyed by a fire. All that was left was smoke and rubble. He asked God why this had happened. He simply couldn't understand it.

Later that day, a ship appeared on the horizon and eventually rescued him. The crew told him they had been plotting a distinct course and had noticed smoke in the distance. They thought the smoke might be a signal for help and had answered the call.[lviii]

The Lord works in mysterious and unexpected ways. So often He answers our prayers and comes to the rescue using events and people we never would have considered. I suspect we all experience seasons where nothing appears to change. This chapter examines how to respond with trust during those seasons.

When God appears to be absent

Many of us have experienced times when God feels absent. The book of Job documents one man's particularly dark season. One moment he had everything a guy could wish for – a wife, children, homes, flocks, servants, health and wealth – and the next moment everything was gone. To add to this, God seemed distant.

"I cry out to you, God, but you do not answer; I stand up, but you merely look at me…Yet when I hoped for good, evil came; when I looked for light, then came darkness" (Job 30:20;26).

Many of us have been through seasons when everything seems to be going wrong, and God appears to have gone AWOL, with no forwarding address! Each day, we call out, "Where are you God?" I have experienced seasons where, like David, I cried out to God over and over again:

"My God, my God, why have you forsaken me?" (see Psalm 22:1).

We must remember that silence isn't absence. God is still very much at work during these times. Even in the silence. Even in the unknown. Even when you can't see any ships on the horizon.

When you don't understand what's going on in your life and God appears silent, remember to keep trusting. He will sometimes allow your faith to be tested, but trust in the One who is faithful, consistent and true; the One who is good all the time. He is not human like us, blessing one day and cursing the next; loving us one day and forgetting us the next. He is trustworthy.

"Your kingdom is an everlasting kingdom, and your dominion endures through all generations. The Lord is trustworthy in all he promises and faithful in all he does" (Psalm 145:13).

When God doesn't answer your prayers

Billy Graham's wife Ruth used to say that if God has answered all her prayers when she was young she would have married the wrong man several times! She often used this story to emphasise this point:

"Two teardrops were floating down the river of life. One asked the other, 'Who are you?' The second teardrop replied, 'I am the teardrop from the girl who loved a man and lost him. Who are you?' The first teardrop replied, 'I am the teardrop of the girl who got him.'"[lix]

We need to be careful what we pray for and be thankful that God doesn't always answer all our prayers in the way we desire. It's so easy to become upset over God's apparent failure to answer when, had He done so, we might be crying even more! Thank God that He knows us better than we know ourselves, and knows what's best for us better than we do. Let's trust Him to straighten out our paths and guide us through life.

When things don't go our way

Julia and I have spent years of our married life in rented accommodation, mainly due to being at Bible College, relocating several times and being on a low income for many years serving God. Once we had established the church in Crewe we started to look for a home to buy. One of the first houses we looked at was a lovely, recently built family home near the church. We fell in love with it immediately. It ticked all the right boxes. We put an offer in, it was accepted, and as we already had a mortgage offer in place we were able to proceed quite quickly.

The next step in the UK is to have a full survey of the house done for the benefit of the lender. Nobody wants to discover an expensive problem once they've moved in. We had visited the house several times and developed a good relationship with the sellers, so we arranged, with their full knowledge, for the survey to be done at the cost of £395, which was a lot of money to us cash-strapped Lawtons. The surveyor completed his survey only for the sellers to inform us later the same day that they had changed their minds about selling. When I called them to ask why they hadn't informed us before we spent the money on the survey they replied that they nearly had that morning but couldn't bring themselves to do so.

To say we were upset at the stupid and thoughtless loss of our money was an understatement. Julia was threatening to put a brick through their front window (not particularly befitting of a pastor's wife, but I have to admit I wasn't far behind in my thinking!) What a complete and needless waste of our precious money for the sake of a phone call.

Sometimes we can feel surprised or shocked when things don't always go our way. However, God had a better plan. A few months later, we quite unexpectedly found a beautiful home in a quiet cul-de-sac, which became or family home for many years. That home has retained a special place in our hearts. God knows best, and if we will only trust Him completely He will make straight paths for our feet. He longs to guide our steps. I can recall countless times when God has quietly, behind the scenes, guided my steps. At times like this we must learn to patiently trust and choose not to throw any bricks!

What to do when nothing appears to be changing

When the referee at a football match makes several apparently bad decisions, English fans often chant: "You don't know what you're doing!" Some of us have had similar thoughts about God at times (don't deny it... We all have if we're honest!). But what should we do when nothing appears to change when we pray, or when we feel like we're not getting any answers?

Here are seven things that might help:

Remember that God is always at work

As I've already said, we sometimes need to remind ourselves of everything God has done in the past. I'm sure there will have been previous occasions when God came through for you suddenly and unexpectedly. We must never forget that He is the God who "turns my darkness into light" (see Psalm 18:28). Turning a light on in a darkened room immediately creates light, and God can suddenly change our situations in like manner.

We're often surprised when our circumstances change unexpectedly, but we must remember that God is constantly working in the background on our behalf. The psalmist reminds us that when we're struggling and need God to intervene, He is invisibly at work, never taking a break:

"I lift up my eyes to the mountains – where does my help come from? My help comes from the Lord, the Maker of heaven and earth. He will not let your foot slip – he who watches over you will not slumber; indeed, he who watches over Israel will neither slumber nor sleep" (Psalm 121:1-4).

So I would encourage you to keep the faith. Trust Him. You have no idea what He is working on in the background on your behalf. You can sleep easy, knowing that your God is working to bring change and transformation to your situation in His perfect timing.

Don't complain!

Julia leads the church's community projects at the Dream Centre, and a couple of years ago I asked her to work an additional day a week because the number of projects and workload had grown. She wasn't sure and would only agree if I was willing to do more around our home. In particular, she requested that I hoover the whole house once a week with the proviso that I did it without being asked and without complaining. I have pretty much managed to fulfil her wishes, although I find the additional clause challenging at times! Who likes hoovering?

Paul encouraged the Philippians to:

"Do everything without complaining and arguing" (Philippians 2:14, NLT).

The Bible classes' whiners and complainers in the same category as ungodly sinners, who live only to satisfy their desires and get what they want (see Jude 15-16). Complaining is so negative, and it appears to be spreading like an epidemic in Britain. We complain about everything from traffic to weather (with due cause at times!) to politicians. Rarely does anyone or anything escape the moans of us Brits. This must stop, as it is unhelpful for the hearer (see Ephesians 4:29) and denies our faith in God for the future.

The Bible tells us that God heard Israel's complaints against Him (see Numbers 11:1-2), and His anger blazed. Our complaints are like accusations against God, whom we profess to have trusted to provide for, protect and guide our lives. Instead, we should: *"Be thankful in all circumstances"* (1 Thessalonians 5:18, NLT). Thanksgiving is the opposite of complaining. It expresses our appreciation for everything God has already done, confidence in what He promises to do, and an assurance that He is in charge.

Praise Him

There is something incredible about praising God during our toughest seasons. While Habakkuk was experiencing such a season, he declared:

"Though the fig-tree does not bud and there are no grapes on the vines, though the olive crop fails and the fields produce no food, though there are no sheep in the sheepfold and no cattle in the stalls, yet I will rejoice in the Lord, I will be joyful in God my Saviour" (Habakkuk 3:17-18).

Praise lifts us beyond our negative thoughts, sends the devil packing, calms our fears, refocuses us on God, brings fresh perspective, and reminds us of who is in charge and what He has done in the past. It recalls His redeeming power, miraculous strength and ability to deliver us from anything at any time. Praise renews our minds, strengthens our hearts, encourages our spirits and enables us to keep going, fully dependant on God.

Make a choice to praise Him no matter how difficult your current situation and outlook is. King Jehoshaphat was being attacked by the Moabites and Ammonites, among others. He made a choice to praise God and give the battle over to Him. The king appointed men to sing to the Lord at the head of the army as they went into battle. He ordered them to praise Him, saying: *"Give thanks to the Lord, for his love endures forever"* (see 2 Chronicles 20:21-22).

As they began to praise, the Lord set ambushes against the enemy troops, and they were defeated. Just imagine the impact your praise and declarations of God's power, splendour and glory could have over your seemingly unchanging situation. Why not swap your pity party for a praise party and see what God will do?

Learn to trust God even more

I recently challenged my congregation about this. I asked them what they do when God doesn't appear to be coming through for them. How should we respond? My answer is this. I pray and simply say to God: "Father, you know that I really trust you. Help me to trust you even more."

When I make this request, God gives me fresh energy, enthusiasm, faith, passion and the ability not to quit in spite of what is going on around me. He has this incredible ability to make weak things strong again. He renews our strength.

Sometimes we have to come to the end of ourselves and just throw ourselves on Him. God always responds to our weakness and humility:

"He gives strength to the weary and increases the power of the weak. Even youths grow tired and weary, and young men stumble and fall; but those who hope in the Lord will renew their strength. They will soar on wings like eagles; they will run and not grow weary, they will walk and not be faint" (Isaiah 40:29-31).

Enjoy the Journey

Sometimes we can be so focused on what we *don't* have that we forget about what we *do* have. There have been times when I have been so stressed and anxious about what needs to change that I miss all that I have already. I had so much on my mind during my early days of ministry that I would be present and yet absent around the home with my wife and kids. When this is the case, you miss the joy of your seeing children grow, learn and have fun. You miss their achievements. You miss out on quality time with your spouse. There is so much to be grateful for and to enjoy. Look for something every day that you can be celebrate. Your eyes will be opened and your mind will be taken off what you ultimately cannot change. Only God can do this, so let Him carry the load.

Finally, brothers, whatever is true, whatever is noble, whatever is right, whatever is pure, whatever is lovely, whatever is admirable—if anything is excellent or praiseworthy—think about such things. Whatever you have learned or received or heard from me, or seen in me—put it into practice. And the God of peace will be with you (Philippians 4:8-9).

In the midst of difficult seasons, we must learn to smile more, enjoy our lives and laugh as much as we can. Sometimes when I'm finding things tough and am tempted to despair, I will watch an old comedy show on TV or read an excerpt from a book that makes me laugh so I can see the funny side of life again. It's a practical way of removing the dogs of doom from my head and choosing to enjoy my life. I have realised that there is always a temptation to become too serious about my life. This is not good, and it doesn't help me to embrace the abundant life Jesus promised.

"Rejoice always, pray continually, give thanks in all circumstances; for this is God's will for you in Christ Jesus" (1 Thessalonians 5:16-18).

Whatever happens, trust!

I'm so encouraged by the story of the three young men in Daniel. These godly young men refused to bow down and worship the gold image Nebuchadnezzar had set up. As a result, they were about to be thrown into the fiery furnace. Nebuchadnezzar challenged them to worship the image, and their reply shows incredible trust in God:

Shadrach, Meshach and Abednego replied to him, 'King Nebuchadnezzar, we do not need to defend ourselves before you in this matter. If we are thrown into the blazing furnace, the God we serve is able to deliver us from it, and he will deliver us from Your Majesty's hand. But even if he does not, we want you to know, Your Majesty, that we will not serve your gods or worship the image of gold you have set up' (Daniel 3:16-18).

In these days of prosperity and 'word of faith' teaching, we must marry great faith with the reality that God knows best for His creation. He has plans and purposes to fulfil, and sometimes we struggle with what He appears to allow. This means that prayers aren't always answered as we anticipate, and we don't always receive what we believe has been promised.

One passage I never hear preached on is a great little passage in Hebrews that talks about the Bible's incredible men and women of faith. The chapter concludes with a narrative about those who suffered and were tortured for their beliefs. It then states:

"These were all commended for their faith, yet none of them received what had been promised, since God had planned something better for us so that only together with us would they be made perfect" (Hebrews 11:39-40).

Like the three young men in Babylon and these other great saints in the Bible, we must make a decision to trust God. I have decided that my faith will never be affected by circumstances or lack. I have resolved to follow Jesus (no turning back), and I will seek to do this with all my heart until I take my final breath. I have chosen to trust Him completely.

Remember that God will never desert you

Welsh minister and leader of the Crusade for World Revival (CWR), Selwyn Hughes, who wrote the outstanding *Every Day with Jesus* daily reading notes, was suffering from prostate cancer when he said this:

"What God allows He also uses. And He never deserts His children, even in the most dire of circumstances, so we can thank Him for that. 'And we know that in all things God works for the good of those who love Him,' said the apostle Paul in Romans 8;28. In all things!"[lx]

God promises never to leave or abandon us. In the days when nothing appears to change, hang on to the promise God gave Joshua as he became leader of Israel (see Deuteronomy 31:8), which is repeated in Hebrews 13:5. Can you imagine what Joshua was facing? God had called him to take over the leadership from Moses. Imagine following in the footsteps of one of the godliest men ever to have lived, and leading the children of Israel (who, let's face it, weren't the easiest, most loyal or obedient group!) in their conquest of the Promised Land where enormous giants and great cities awaited.

God promised Joshua that He would be with him just as He had been with Moses (see Joshua 1:5), and that He would never leave him or abandon him. The same promise applies to you and to me. God is with us no matter what we face.

The Lord is my light and my salvation — whom shall I fear? The Lord is the stronghold of my life — of whom shall I be afraid? When the wicked advance against me to devour me, it is my enemies and my foes who will stumble and fall. Though an army besiege me, my heart will not fear; though war break out against me, even then I will be confident (Psalm 27:1-3).

Imagine

As we close this chapter, I want to encourage you once again to trust God like never before. Some will have jumped straight to this chapter when they spotted it in the Contents. Such is your situation that you're struggling to continue to trust God and feel like giving up on your faith. Perhaps your current circumstances have continued for so long you've just accepted they will never change. Don't give up hope! Against all the odds, Abraham believed and became the father of nations. The enemy would love to rob you of your hope and cause you to relinquish your trust in God. Resist him. Don't quit. Determine to keep going.

Ask Him to renew your hope and give you the strength to keep going. Make a choice to be joyful, to focus on what you have, to celebrate all that God has done and enjoy the journey. Make the choice to trust Him completely, whatever that means for you, until your final breath.

Chapter 13

In the major decisions

In 1986, I met Julia at a mother and toddler group attached to our home church. What a romantic place with toys, crying babies, dirty nappies and screaming kids everywhere! I was serving as an intern, and she had three boys under the age of five. I was actually engaged to be married to someone else at the time, but something drew me to her and I have never, even for one moment, regretted asking Julia to be my wife. She has been an absolutely incredible partner, mother and church leader. Much of what we are achieving now at the Dream Centre stems from her hard work, faith and creativity.

During the early months of our relationship, we were both very aware that Julia's young boys had already lost one dad. I felt enormous pressure to 'hear from God' as to whether we should be together permanently. I didn't want the boys growing to accept me as their dad and then losing another father figure. We split up twice during those early months.

I won Julia back the second time by bringing two iced buns with me when I called round to see her (I was a guy of limited means!), and somehow it was enough to get a result. As time went by we began to realise that we were meant to be together and, once married, with all its inevitable challenges, we both had to trust God that marriage was what He had planned and purposed for us. Looking back, I'm so glad we chose each other.

Over the past three decades of married life, we have had to make many big decisions: following the call to ministry, planting a church, deciding whether to have a fifth child, purchasing homes and church buildings, leaving our children and the church we had planted behind, and relocating to the northeast of England. The list goes on.

Another child?

Let me take you back to the early spring of 1992 and our decision to have a fifth child. We were at Bible college and money was incredibly tight. We already had four children, and Julia and I were having the conversation so many parents have: should we have another? I had made up my mind that, as much as I loved our kids and would have loved a fifth, four were more than enough to look after and we couldn't afford another child at that point.

We spoke about this on several occasions, and one day Julia said to me: "Have you asked God what we should do? You ask Him about all the other major decisions you make." I have to admit I had taken the decision out of His hands and made my own call.

So I prayed about it and felt God encourage me to trust Him to make the final call. I told Julia that I had agreed with God that she had six months to become pregnant, and after that I would have a vasectomy (it makes me wince just typing the word!). By the early summer Julia was pregnant, and our beautiful daughter Amy was born in February 1994.

God provided for us miraculously during those early years. Amy never went without, as a generous family member constantly gave us designer baby clothes for her. Amy was one of the best-dressed babies around! More importantly, those who know her will know that she has a beautiful nature and has been an incredible blessing, not just to our family, but to our church and as an early years teacher at a local school. I shudder to think what we would have missed out on had I stubbornly refused to trust God in this decision. It was another big lesson for me.

We've got to learn to hear God's voice

In order to trust God in the major decisions of life, we must learn to hear and discern His voice. God has promised that if we trust Him continually and talk to Him about our plans, He will make our paths straight.

"The Lord says, 'I will guide you along the best pathway for your life. I will advise you and watch over you. Do not be like a senseless horse or mule that needs a bit and bridle to keep it under control.' Many

sorrows come to the wicked, but unfailing love surrounds those who trust the Lord" (Psalms 32:8-10, NLT).

There's no way that any of us want to be like that senseless horse or mule. So how do we receive this guidance, especially when it concerns major decisions? How do we discover His plans for our lives?

"My sheep hear My voice, and I know them, and they follow Me" (John 10:27, NKJV).

Hearing from God is so critical. Trusting Him is completely dependent on us hearing His voice clearly. As a pastor, I have lost count of the times someone has sat in my office and told me that God has told them to do something. But when I have challenged them to share the evidence with me, they rarely have more to say than: "Well I've prayed about it a lot and I feel this is right." My response is to share with them the methods I use when I seek God for guidance. Then I ask them to go away and pray for a few weeks, and tell them we'll meet up again when they have done so.

The danger with all this is that we are so often at the mercy of our thoughts and desires, and we can also come under the attack of the enemy, who wants to rob us of our destiny in Christ. I have had Christians tell me that God has told them to step down from a ministry they love during a challenging season, leave the church, live with a partner, marry an unsaved partner, give up the job of their dreams during a tough patch or that they don't need to forgive someone. I have heard it all!

The big question many Christians ask is this: how do I know I've heard from God? I would reply that, in my experience, if we allow Him plenty of time and opportunity to speak, He *will* speak. Let's look at some ways of preparing ourselves to hear God's voice.

Develop your relationship with God
There is no substitute for spending time with God, or for getting to know His voice and the specific ways He speaks to each one of us. Within the routine of our busy lives we need to take time out to be quiet and listen, particularly when major decisions need to be made.

"Talk in prayer is essential but it is also partial. Silence is also essential" (Eugene Petersen).[lxi]

Joyce Huggett's classic book, *Listening to God*, is well worth reading. In it, she shares the different ways God speaks to us and the ways people hear Him (we're all different). She also explores how we can tune our spirits to hear His voice.

When I was at Bible college, I used to block off Friday mornings from nine a.m. to noon so I could learn to listen to God's voice. I would shut myself away and put a note on our apartment door saying: 'Do not disturb.' I learned to worship, quieten my heart from all distracting voices and sit quietly as I waited for God to start speaking to me about my life, character, sin and studies, and about His future plans.

"Prayer is not monologue, but dialogue. Its most essential part is God's voice in response to mine" (Andrew Murray).[lxii]

One of the verses I have really come to love is Jeremiah 33:3:

"Call to me and I will answer you and tell you great and unsearchable things you do not know."

I have found that God has countless things to share with me that I am not presently aware of, and that, if I seek Him, He will bring wisdom, revelation and insight into my life, family and ministry.

I remember a time when Julia and I were having difficulties with someone who was causing real problems; so much so that the stress and anxiety had affected Julia's sleep and caused her hair to start falling out. We were caught in what seemed like a catch-22 situation, but if we will only seek Him, God always provides a way where there seems to be no other way. He showed us exactly what to do, and this massive problem was soon resolved to everyone's satisfaction.

At other times there have been seemingly unsolvable problems in ministry, challenging situations with our children, demonic attacks, financial challenges and other situations when only wisdom and revelation from heaven will help. God has been faithful to His promises. He has continually revealed things we didn't know at the time and shown us how to bring about a positive solution.

Pray, pray, pray!
Many Christians are weedy prayers! Sorry if this cause's offence, but so few of us have learned how to "pray through" as RA Torrey put it.[lxiii] We maybe pray once or twice, or more regularly for a few days, but if we don't immediately feel that anything has happened we can lose interest. We need to learn to really pray things through.

When I'm seriously seeking God, that matter will stay close to my heart, and will be one of the first things I mention in my regular conversations with God each day. I will raise it with Him several times a day. It will be written at the top of my 'to do' list to remind me that it's important. I will create moments when I sit quietly and ask God to speak to me.

Prayer cannot be rushed. Seeking God for clear guidance takes time, but you can create these moments while driving, waiting for an appointment, in the shower, washing up, or even when you're hoovering (note to self!). If you give God every opportunity to speak, He will do so.

God will speak even when you're not listening
Since attuning myself to God's voice, I have found that He will speak to me even when I'm (being polite and reverent here) not specifically praying or asking Him to speak. Several years ago, I was attending a leadership conference at Life Church in Bradford. During one of the breaks I was sitting on the steps looking out across the city as I enjoyed my coffee, and my eyes were drawn towards the line of coaches and minibuses parked in front of me. God spoke clearly to me: "If you pray and ask me to give you one of those minibuses, I will do it."

We had just started transporting some vulnerable women and children from various parts of the town to our church services, but I hadn't considered the church actually owning a minibus. We had no budget for anything like that.

I walked down the steps and took note of the minibus in front of me: a seventeen-seater LDV Convoy. I felt God say to me: "This is between you and me. Don't mention it to anyone else or make any appeal for funds. Simply pray and ask me."

About a month later, a Christian man I had never met before rang me and said that God had told him to look for someone who needed help with minibuses, and that he had found my name in the telephone directory. He refurbished these minibuses and sold them on to Christian organisations. He wanted £3,500 for the one he had. Naturally, we didn't have the money to purchase one, so I told him I would contact him once I'd prayed the money in.

To cut a long story short, the same man contacted me after several months of privately praying like I'd never prayed before to ask if he could call in and see me as he was on his way to deliver a minibus to a friend. To my shock and delight, I was that friend! We had never met before and here was this guy giving me, completely free of charge, a refurbished seventeen-seater LDF Convoy with a new engine!

God is amazing. If we will learn to listen, He will speak to us at unexpected moments, bringing revelation, wisdom, guidance, blessing and provision.

Read His Word every day
"Your word is a lamp to guide my feet and a light for my path" (Psalms 119:105, NLT).

When we neglect to read His Word, we will struggle to make major decisions. He has blessed us with His incredible, guiding Word. If you don't already, I would really encourage you to follow a reading plan and read a portion of the Bible every day. Here's why:

First, it's incredible how many 'coincidences' occur when we are disciplined in this. How does the Holy Spirit – who, incidentally, Jesus promised would *"lead us into all truth"* (see John 16:13) – manage to coordinate this? How many times have you heard other Christians say: "I was reading my Bible today, and it was exactly what I needed to read?"

Second, when we regularly read His Word, we get it into our spirit. The Holy Spirit then reminds us of what God has already said in His Word when we seek Him about major decisions. I have a poor memory, but the Holy Spirit provides this incredible power of recall when I seek Him. It's astounding what I can remember with His help.

The truth with God is that He will never, ever contradict what He has already revealed through His Word, and believe me I've had people sit in my office and argue with me about this one. Someone who had only just come out of a disastrous marriage with an unbeliever, and who in my opinion was on the 'rebound', asked me to pray about whether they should remarry a second unbeliever. I refused and said that I wasn't going to waste my or God's time asking Him to answer a question that He has clearly provided in His Word. Paul could not have been clearer: *"Do not be yoked together with unbelievers..."* (2 Corinthians 6:14). Sadly, this person ignored my advice, left the church and ended up in another unhappy marriage.

Take your time and weigh up the pros and cons
God is never in the rush we are in to make decisions. If we took a little bit longer when making major decisions, particularly in those that are going to impact and change lives, we would be better for it. We need to take time to ask Him and then listen.

Julia often gets cross with me because I'll ask her a question but not listen to the answer because, while the question was important, I'm too engrossed in getting on with what I'm doing to wait for the answer! Impatience is not one of the gifts of the Spirit. Let's learn to slow the process down and allow God to speak.

I've also found that weighing up the pros and cons can really help in bringing clarity to our decision-making. There have been several occasions when I have been quite keen to make a major change in my life or ministry, and I've found simply listing the positives and negatives brings a different perspective. It shouldn't be the only method we use, but it can save us a lot of time. At the end of the day, God wants us to use our common sense as well as praying and seeking His face.

Give God the opportunity to close a door
When we were in the final negotiation stage of purchasing the Dream Centre, I was pretty convinced that we were doing the right thing, but not everyone in our church was. I understood this because it was a

massive decision with major implications for the future. I also knew that not everyone had been as involved as our leaders and experienced, close at hand, the journey of hearing God's voice and seeing God move as we had. So we called a meeting to share the journey, allowing people to ask questions and process what was occurring.

One of the things I encouraged people with was the story in Acts concerning the debate among the Pharisees about the powerful impact of the early believers' ministry. They were setting Jerusalem on fire with their teaching and miracles and had been thrown in prison as a result. The angel of the Lord had just miraculously released them. The Pharisees were furious and had resolved to kill the believers. However, Gamaliel, a respected expert in the law, discouraged his colleagues from taking action:

"So my advice is, leave these men alone. Let them go. If they are planning and doing these things merely on their own, it will soon be overthrown. But if it is from God, you will not be able to overthrow them. You may even find yourselves fighting against God!" (Acts 5:38-39, NLT).

I used the story to encourage them that I believed the move was of God, but that if it wasn't we were convinced that He was more than capable of closing the door. I also said that if we fought against it and God *was* behind the move, we could find ourselves fighting God. That's never a great move! Our people were very supportive and encouraged us to continue with our preparations and plans.

Just recently, I was about to have a conversation with a member of my church that was not going to be easy. I had spent some considerable time praying, reflecting and checking with God that I was doing the right thing. Such was my concern that the night before I had said to God: "This is really serious now. Father, if I'm in the wrong or if I'm being led into wrong thinking by my own tiredness, weariness or frustrations, please show me and I won't go ahead with the conversation. You need to speak to me." God confirmed that I was on the right track and, while difficult, the conversation went ahead and proved the right thing to do.

Maybe you're applying for a job or accepting a new position. I would encourage you to do it with prayerful caution, saying: "God, I think this is right, but please close the door if it isn't. Show me. Speak to me. Use someone else to speak into my life. Don't let me stray from the right path for my life."

Look for confirmation from independent sources

It's so tempting to use Bible reading notes like a horoscope. Have you ever looked ahead to a critical day in your life and read the notes (yes, I have too!). It's not great practice. Sometimes we're tempted to make major decisions based on the flimsiest pieces of guidance. We need more than that. My prayer is: "Father, show me through independent people and different mediums (not literally mediums; that's not good practice either!) Your will in this situation." I've found that God is more than capable of revealing His will if I ask Him, but also that He's not usually in any rush.

In August 2013, the elders of our church and I went on a prayer retreat to seek God about our next move. We had been deliberating about employing another member of staff or whether to purchase the Dream Centre. We were really unclear in our minds, so we devoted the day to praying and fasting.

At one point, having felt God speak clearly about buying the centre, I encouraged each elder to go off into the grounds for an hour or so to seek confirmation. When they returned, each elder came back with the same picture of an open door.

During the period when we were negotiating with the owner, so many visiting speakers had the same picture. I remember three of my friends individually starting their messages with the same image. They would say something like this: "I don't normally receive pictures from God, but I have to share this. I keep seeing this picture of an open door!"

God confirms His Word. The decision to swap the original church building for an enormous, rundown, four-storey bingo hall, which needed a complete refurbishment from top to bottom, was a massive one. It was a scary concept with far-reaching implications. I remember standing in the main corridor moments after I had received the call from our solicitor to say we had completed the deal, wondering to myself, "Simon, what have you done?"

Several years on, I have no regrets. The new centre has created many new challenges, which have required more trust and faith than ever before, but hundreds of lives have been impacted and changed, and many have come to Christ. We must continue to trust God and not despise the day of small things (see Zechariah 4:10).

If we will trust God with all our hearts, we will be patient, because trust involves waiting at times. Impatient people show a lack of trust in others. I remember waiting for an answer after being interviewed for Bible college. Every day at lunchtime I would find a call box and ring Julia to ask if we had received an acceptance letter. Today I wouldn't be making that call. I would be patiently waiting, trusting that God knows best for my life and will make my paths straight. He can also be totally trusted with your life.

"But I am trusting you, O Lord, saying, 'You are my God!' My future is in your hands..." (Psalms 31:14-15, NLT).

Peace when making major decisions
In my experience, the longer we have been Christians the more we sense what God is saying and calling us to do. Just as couples who have been married for years begin to instinctively and almost telepathically know what the other is thinking or would want to do in a situation, we can become attuned to what God would say or want us to do.

It also becomes much easier to hear and recognise His voice over time. I'm always concerned when I don't have a sense of peace about a decision or direction. While it's often impossible to feel one hundred percent sure that you're making the right decision, I expect to experience a strong sense of peace when I'm making big calls. If I don't, I will hold fire or revisit it later.

We all have the indwelling Holy Spirit as our counsellor and guide. I believe that if we have invested in our relationship with God and spent time with Him, He will reveal His will. More often than not, we will experience a sense of peace and assurance from the Holy Spirit that we are on the right track.

Whenever we believe we have heard from God and make a big decision, doubts and anxieties will creep in. The enemy of our faith will come knocking at the door of our minds and try to plant fear there. At these times we must learn to ignore such thoughts and trust God with everything we have. We can ask God to help us trust. The disciples asked Jesus to increase their faith (see Luke 17:5), and we must not be afraid to ask Him to increase our trust after making big decisions.

Sometimes we feel we could never achieve the same levels of trust the biblical heroes of faith had. How could we ever trust God like Moses, Elijah or Paul? Yet my reading of the narrative of their lives is that they were on a journey of trust just like us. None of them became instant 'superheroes of faith'. They all had moments of doubt and anxiety but discovered, with God's help, how to trust Him more in each and every experience they went through. If we can learn to trust God and hear His voice clearly, who knows what God will do in and through us in the future?

"...The people who know their God shall be strong, and carry out great exploits" (Daniel 11:32).

Imagine
As I look back on my life I can see that God has been leading me and guiding me, often without me being aware. In my early days as a Christian it was really hard to hear His voice, but as I've learned from Him and invested more time in the relationship I've learned to hear His voice more clearly as I make major calls. If your heart is surrendered to Him, and you take your time, soaking important decisions in prayer, He will lead and guide you.

I've also found that God looks for us to show a basic level of trust and to start moving in the direction in which He is calling us. It is then that the confirmations begin to arrive and further guidance occurs. God doesn't want us to just sit on our hands and wait for Him to do something. Can I encourage you to take some steps in the direction you believe God is calling you into? What could you do now that would create an opportunity for God to confirm that you're on the right path? Why not ask Him? Imagine where this could lead...

Chapter 14

With your future

Civil rights advocate Ralph Abernathy said: *"I don't know what the future holds, but I do know who holds the future."*[lxiv]

I remember when God called me to ministry. I was only twenty-two, and at the time I was very much enjoying my career at one of the UK's largest stationery and book chains. I loved working for this major retailer and, having already received two promotions, I was only a step away from my initial ambition of becoming a store manager.

However, God had other plans. He didn't want me to build stores; He wanted me to build His Kingdom. This meant taking a massive step of faith. It involved giving up my job, career aspirations and future to head home to Leicester and serve as an intern, at least to begin with, at my local church.

I was based near Norfolk prior to the move and attended a small church in the tiny village of Tydd Gote near Wisbech. I had been praying a great deal that God would give me the confirmation I needed about giving up my career. He had done so much in my life and I wanted to share it with others. One particular morning in late November 1985, I was chatting to one of the guys at the back of the church after the service. When I went to collect my Bible, which I had accidentally left in the pew, I noticed it was open, and there was a verse underlined:

"Jesus did not let him, but said, 'Go home to your own people and tell them how much the Lord has done for you, and how he has had mercy on you'" (Mark 5:19).

To this day, I have no idea why my Bible was open at that page or why that verse was underlined. The pastor hadn't been preaching on it, and I couldn't remember underlining it. Had an angel with a pen been at work? Whatever way it happened, this confirmed everything I had sensed God was calling me to do. A few weeks later, I resigned my position – much to my area manager's shock (and derision) – to follow the call of God.

Stepping out in faith

Stepping out in faith is always a challenge. If we're really going to trust God with all our hearts, we will have to do this on occasion. It could be the challenge to lead a team, increase your giving or apply for a new job. It will mean hearing from God, trusting Him and taking that first step of faith. I've watched many Christians struggle with this over the years, and I can understand why. When God challenges us to take a faith step, it can be daunting. It will often require commitment, sacrifice, risk, time and the loss of something we value or enjoy.

Julia and I knew that our time in Crewe was coming to an end in 2006, and when the opportunity to relocate to a church in Newcastle came up in the summer of 2008 we were excited and fearful at the same time. It was a massive move for us and would mean separation from our children, whom we love dearly. We also anticipated that we would miss out on seeing any future grandchildren regularly.

Yet we knew and recognised the call of God to move. We just knew it was Him. Everything pointed to it, and after the interview I believe God spoke to me quite clearly that the confirmations would come after I accepted the position. There were only three days between the interview and the offer. The church wanted an answer, so we arrived at Elim's national conference and took up the offer. Over the course of the next week, three different people, on three separate occasions, gave us the Newcastle church's mission statement verse (Isaiah 54:2-3) in either words or prayers. God confirms His call when we trust Him.

"Whether you turn to the right or to the left, your ears will hear a voice behind you, saying, 'This is the way; walk in it'" (Isaiah 30:21).

As I look at what God has trusted me with since that time, and trusts me with today, I can only imagine what I would have missed out on had I refused to trust Him then. Every time I have chosen to trust, I have found that He has entrusted me with even more.

Trusting God as you step out

Pastor and author Naeem Callaway is quoted as saying: *"Sometimes the smallest step in the right direction ends up being the biggest step of your life. Tiptoe if you must, but take a step."*[lxv]

One of the most exciting and fulfilling things we can do in life is to step out and do something we have never done before for God. I'm often a sounding board for members of my congregation as they consider stepping out of their comfort zones into new jobs, relationships, career opportunities and new ministries. Many have discovered that it's incredibly fulfilling to:

- Volunteer for the first time and give something back
- Use their God-given passion, heart, gifts, abilities and experiences to help others
- Create something new, such as a book or a first worship song
- Lead a church meeting
- Build a new team or start a ministry
- Establish a new small group
- See something they have launched begin to grow
- Mentor a young person and watch them mature
- Build a business and use the profits for the Kingdom

Surely when you come to the end of your days you don't want to look back at your life and realise you have played it safe, focusing on survival rather than fulfilling God's purpose. There has to be more to life that...

Ask yourself the following questions:

- What would I really love to do? What is my passion?
- What would I do if I knew I couldn't fail, or if I was guaranteed to succeed?
- What could I do for God tomorrow if I trusted Him more today?

I want to inspire you to live out your dream, and if you don't already have one, ask God to give you one!

Author Rusty Rustenbach writes: *"You and I live in an age when only a rare minority of individuals desire to spend their lives in pursuit of objectives which are bigger than they are. In our age, for most people, when they die it will be as though they never lived."*[lxvi]

Trust God and step out promptly when He directs you to do so. He will often allow the enemy to test you when you take a giant step of faith. Opposition will undoubtedly come when you choose to follow God and do whatever He has called you to do. It's rarely an easy time, but the results far outweigh the challenges.

Discovering God's faithfulness as you step out
There have been many times in my life when I have discovered God's amazing faithfulness, particularly when I have stepped out and obeyed Him. It seems to me that God is looking for men and women who will really trust and take risks for Him; who believe His Word and stand on it. All it takes is the small measure of faith God has already placed in you to get started, and then watch where He takes you. One of the keys is to do precisely what He has told you to do now. Just. Do. It. Yes, now!

I have a theory that there must have been occasions in my life when I genuinely believed I had heard God's voice, trusted Him and stepped out, yet was wrong. This possibly created questioning conversations in heaven; but help and assistance was provided nevertheless. God chose to bless my endeavours in any case. Such is the heart of God for His children.

When we step out, God steps in
I believe God absolutely loves it when we really trust Him and step out in faith. I often say to people: "When we step out, God steps in." He loves people of faith who don't just talk a great game but are willing to get onto the field and play the game.

We have seen this so many times in our church. When we bought the Dream Centre, we had no idea where the money or the people we needed to establish the new ministries would come from, yet God has provided every step of the way. I often say to my congregation that God didn't say to me: "Here's a million pounds. Find something to spend it on!" Rather, He said: "Here's a building. Buy it and I'll do the rest." Over the last three years, we have seen miracle after miracle. Yes, it's been tough and challenging at times, but God has provided in ways we never expected. The job is far from finished, but we're on a journey of faith and are learning to trust Him more every day.

Waiting for the starting pistol

King David came from the sheep pen to become Israel's king, but it wasn't an easy or straightforward journey. God's plan involved many years of preparation and training for the man who would lead Israel. The training involved rearing and protecting sheep, ducking Saul's spears, living as a fugitive in caves, working with and developing a group of six hundred dysfunctional misfits, and learning to wait for God's timing and schedule.

Anointed king in his teens, David had to wait until he was thirty to become Judah's ruler and a little longer to become king of all Israel. Don't despise the preparation time. Instead, learn to trust God's perfect timing. A wonderful prize awaits those who are committed to trusting God over the long haul.

As American pastor and author, Bob Gass, writes:

"Waiting is hard, but if you run before the starter fires the gun, you'll be disqualified from the race and never receive the prize."[lxvii]

During the seasons of waiting for the future promise to materialise, we have to keep trusting God. We must avoid forcing the door and creating an Ishmael (see Genesis 16). We have to learn to wait patiently.

There have been times in my life when I have simply had to entrust God with the future. During my final two years serving as pastor of the church we had planted in Crewe some eleven years earlier, I knew with absolute certainty that our time there was drawing to a close. I had run out of vision and needed a fresh challenge. Equally importantly, the church there needed a new pastor with a fresh vision!

It was a tough two years being in limbo, but I just had to keep believing and wait patiently for His perfect timing. I continued to knuckle down and worked hard at what was in front of me, and what God had called me to do during that season. Amazingly, God had sown a seed in my heart eighteen months before we eventually moved to Newcastle, and I sensed that one day we would lead a church there.

Whether it's a dream job, promotion, ministry opportunity, relationship, debt release, first home or healing, your strength is in quietness and trust. Learn to patiently trust the One who has your life in His more than capable hands.

Trusting God when the door doesn't open

We also need to be careful to identify when God is present in an opportunity or desire to do something. Lots of exciting opportunities have arisen during my life that have not been from God, and I have been left disappointed when a door that was partially opened suddenly closed. But I've learned that when God shuts a door I need to stop banging on it! Trust God that whatever is behind it wasn't meant for you. We will probably never know until eternity why God didn't answer all our prayers or open certain doors, but I imagine we will be incredibly grateful when we find out. God knows best.

Wisdom often comes with age, and one of things I have learned over the years is that we can completely rely on God to open the right doors for us. I would far rather He opened the door than try to force it open with a crowbar myself! This is why it's so important not to lean on our limited understanding, but rather to trust in His complete knowledge.

The older I get, the more frequently doors of opportunity appear to open for me. Maybe it's because I'm learning to surrender my future to Him and allowing Him to guide my life. I know that His hand is on the steering wheel. But sometimes He will let us have our own way just to show that He knows best.

Be fully prepared for doors to open

During my final few years in Crewe, God told me quite clearly that I needed to start restructuring the church. Over a couple of years, I studied, researched, discussed and created a new structure. But I knew in my spirit that I was preparing for the next challenge, and we had only just finalised the new structure when we left for Newcastle.

We're not in charge of opening doors, but it's our responsibility to make sure we're ready when God opens them. Funnily enough, during my interview for the Newcastle role, the elders emphasised that the priority for the new pastor, whoever that might be, would be to restructure the church. Nothing is wasted! God uses every experience and season as a learning experience for what He has planned next. By the time the Newcastle opportunity became available, I was ready for it. In fact, God prepared my heart and mind for what lay ahead. Sometimes He waits until He knows we're ready for what is coming.

"Until the time came to fulfil his dreams, the Lord tested Joseph's character" (Psalms 105:19, NLT).

Like Joseph, I'm sure God was working on other aspects of my character and leadership approach during this period. He rarely moves us into the next appointment until we are ready. The wise person learns to embrace what God is doing in his or her life. God knows best, and the better prepared we are for the next adventure the more successful we will be.

No regrets

I sometimes meet Christians who are living regret-filled lives. They have missed out on opportunities God presented because they refused to trust Him when they heard Him calling their names. When we fail to step out in faith, we always end up missing out. God's purposes will stand. He is looking for men and women who will take risks for Him. If that person is not you or me, He will use the next available person to build His Kingdom and change lives.

I have made a decision that I will, as far as I am able, end my days with no regrets. When I'm sitting in my armchair with my 'pipe and slippers', and my life is almost over, I don't want to regret missing out on any opportunities God has given me by failing to walk through the doors He has opened. It will be too late then. I have resolved to follow Jesus and trust Him as much as I possibly can. It goes without saying that I'm far from perfect and am on the same journey of trust as any other believer, but I'm making a concerted effort to travel in the right direction.

Imagine

I remain absolutely convinced that, if we will completely trust God, new adventures will arise, doors will open, experiences will be shared, lives will be changed, relationships will be enjoyed, and we will live life in all its abundance. My regular prayer is this: "God, open new doors of opportunity. Take me on some new adventures!"

In order to prepare, how about taking some time out to pray and seek God? Then write down a personal vision for your life and your next steps. Vision must move from imagination to action, so break your dream down into goals and take that first step.

Chapter 15

When you feel fearful

It was a beautiful, crisp December morning in the Midwest. Julia and I had said our fond farewells to my wonderful American family, having just enjoyed our first ever Thanksgiving in Omaha. Our first flight was a relatively short one to Chicago, and we were both looking forward to getting up in the air and enjoying the start of what would be a long journey home to the UK.

The pilot welcomed us onto the flight with the news that we could be in for a rather bumpy ride to Chicago, and that not only would there be no in-flight refreshments, but that we should all (flight crew included) stay in our seats with our seat belts fastened at all times. It's always a little disarming when a pilot gives you that kind of information, and he was correct in that there was quite a storm as we started our descent into Chicago. Thunder, lightning, wind and rain filled the early evening darkness.

At times like this you have to remind yourself that the pilot is highly experienced and has taken this flight path many times before in similar conditions. Besides, Chicago is renowned for its wind, storms and delayed flights. More importantly, we can make the decision to trust in the One who has the plane in His more than capable hands and put our faith in Him when we're feeling fearful.

I know people who have an incredible fear of flying and refuse to travel anywhere by plane. This places such a restriction on their lives. Imagine all that they are missing out on: the new countries, the breath-taking scenery, the new vistas, the relationships with people overseas, the challenges, the experiences and the God-created opportunities. Flying opens the door to the rest of the world!

There are many occasions in our lives when we can feel afraid. It might be when we suddenly receive bad news, a change in our circumstances or the opportunity to step out into the new thing God has called us to. However, we must learn to put aside those fears and 'get on the plane'.

I wonder what your greatest fear is....
I must admit that I'm a bit fearful of heights and confined spaces, and have always struggled with a fear of death since being in hospital as a child. It's not death itself that frightens me, but dying before my time and leaving my family bereaved.

Maybe you share the same fears, or maybe it's something else, such as flying, darkness, spiders, unemployment, failure, the future, the unknown, embarrassment, rejection, losing everything, commitment, a person (boss, colleague, family member or 'friend'), sickness, old age or being alone.

"Surely God is my salvation; I will trust and not be afraid. The Lord, the Lord himself, is my strength and my defence; he has become my salvation" (Isaiah 12:2).

God doesn't want us to be fearful or afraid. He wants us to really trust Him. The devil, on the other hand, wants to make us fearful, and will convince us to be afraid of all kinds of things.

What has the enemy has convinced you of?
The enemy loves to sow seeds of fear and cause us to distrust God. He will lie to you and tell you:

- You will never be happy
- Your life is pointless
- Any sickness you have is cancer
- Your life is over
- You can't break that habit or addiction
- You cannot move on from your past. It will haunt you and hold you back forever!
- God could never forgive you
- You can't do that
- You'll always be single
- You'll never be able to have children

- You'll never feel one hundred percent again
- You'll always be in debt
- You're not loved
- You'll get the same disease your parent had

What has the enemy convinced you of? What are you fearful about right now? Let's not forget that God has called us to trust Him with all our hearts, despite how we feel or what we fear. He is in control. Completely in control. Our lives are in His hands. I remember seeing a poster that said:

"The only thing we have to fear is fear itself" (Franklin D. Roosevelt). Someone had added underneath it: *"And sharks"* (one-legged surfer). I love that!

The impact of fear
Fear has wide-ranging implications in our lives. It:

- Steals life, faith, trust, hope, joy, peace, contentment, confidence, boldness to obey, courage, creativity and thinking power, robbing us of the rewards of faith.
- Immobilises us, limiting and often halting destiny in its tracks, and stopping us being all God has called us to be. It brings containment to our lives. It stops us taking risks, stepping out in faith, growing, fulfilling God's plans and purpose for our lives, witnessing, serving, giving and so on. Remember that only Simon Peter experienced walking on water. The other guys were too fearful to give it a go. I reckon I would have been right in there!
- Controls and destroys lives. If allowed to, fear will take over our minds causing anxiety, worry, behavioural problems, sleeplessness, stress, and emotional responses leading to additional physical problems, including shaking, tremors, twitching, cold sweats and other physical symptoms. If unabated, it has the power to oppress, control, torment and torture us. It's horrible. I've been there.

The source of all fear

It doesn't come from God, but rather from the other fella! Fear is: "False Evidence Appearing Real." It can appear very real at times! Fear is falsehood, and it comes from the devil, who is the enemy of our souls, the father of lies, and the destroyer of our peace (see John 8:44).

Jesus warned that the devil comes to kill, steal and destroy (see John 10:10). He loves to spread fear, and he uses lies to deceive God's people and cause us to be fearful. However, as Paul reminded Timothy:

"...God has not given us a spirit of fear, but of power and of love and of a sound mind" (2 Timothy 1:7, NKJV).

Be encouraged!

All the major 'characters' in the Bible were fearful at times, but God didn't allow them dwell there for long. His desire is that we would all live without fear:

'But you, Israel, my servant, Jacob, whom I have chosen, you descendants of Abraham my friend, I took you from the ends of the earth, from its farthest corners I called you. I said, "You are my servant"; I have chosen you and have not rejected you. So do not fear, for I am with you; do not be dismayed, for I am your God. I will strengthen you and help you; I will uphold you with my righteous right hand' (Isaiah 41:8-10).

God said to Israel: *"Do not fear!"* Why? Because He was with them. Consider that for a moment. Why shouldn't we fear? Because God is with us! There is no room for fear. Be encouraged as you read that passage again. The great 'I am' is with you.

Trusting God means mastering fear

"Surely the righteous will never be shaken; they will be remembered for ever. They will have no fear of bad news; their hearts are steadfast,

trusting in the LORD. Their hearts are secure, they will have no fear; in the end they will look in triumph on their foes" (Psalm 112:6-8).

I remember my childhood bath times. They were great! I loved playing with my toy boats in the bath. My father would put a small amount of shampoo on my head, then pour a bit of water on my head to make a lather.

As soon as he did that, I would tip my head down and the water and shampoo would go in my eyes, stinging them. No matter how many times my dad told me to keep my head up and look straight at him, my reaction was the same every time. Fear overruled the trust I had in my father.

This is so like our relationship with God. I know that God is my Father, and I'm certain that He loves me. But sometimes in a difficult situation I panic and turn my eyes away from Him. That never works. I just become more afraid, and the shampoo blinds me! Our lack of trust hurts God, but it hurts us even more. We suffer real pain.

How can we master fear?
American author Mark Twain wrote: *"Courage is resistance to fear, mastery of fear – not absence of fear."*[lxviii]

When the enemy comes in like a flood and attempts to make us fearful, we must be prepared to take a stand and fight for our present and our future. This will take courage and a willingness to master our fears. Below are some of the ways that have helped me do this.

Recognise his schemes
Satan is the deceiver, and he is an incredibly convincing one. He has a tailor-made scheme for each of us! Paul recognised this:

"Anyone you forgive, I also forgive. And what I have forgiven—if there was anything to forgive—I have forgiven in the sight of Christ for your sake, in order that Satan might not outwit us. For we are not unaware of his schemes" (2 Corinthians 2:10-11).

Unforgiveness is one such scheme the enemy will try to entrap us with, and if he is allowed to this can cause considerable damage. However, this is only one of his schemes. From experience, I believe he first identifies our weaknesses and then picks on them. Just as he had a strategy for Jesus in the wilderness, he has a strategy for you and me.

Fear is another massive scheme. He will whisper lies, deceptions, speculative thoughts and negative predictions that have the potential to become strongholds of the mind, which can eventually control and dictate our thinking. The subject matter will normally involve something that is really important to you, for example your health, future, job, relationship, money or family.

According to Kris Vallotton in *Spirit Wars*, a leading university study revealed that the average person hears twelve hundred words of self-talk per minute. Around eleven hundred are negative for most people!

"Speculations prey upon our fears, seeking open doors in our lives through which they can lead us into bondage" (Kris Vallotton).[lxix]

Can I encourage you to recognise the scheme he has placed in your life? What does he regularly use to trip you up and bring you down with? Remember that he comes to steal, kill and destroy.

The devil left Jesus alone until an opportune time. He doesn't play fair, and will often wait until we're tired, hungry and weak to pounce. We need to be alert to Satan's plans and ways. He will often attack when we are on the verge of a breakthrough, or almost at the fulfilment of a dream, to try to make us give up. I have found that fear often rears its ugly head when I'm about to take new ground or embark on a new project. It's almost as if the moment I stick my head above the parapet the arrows start flying in. Thank God for the shield of faith with which I can extinguish all the flaming arrows that come my way. I've that learned during these times of intense attack I simply have to trust God and step out into all that He has called me to do.

I'm convinced that Nehemiah was fearful when he returned to build the walls of Jerusalem. The enemy threw everything at him in an attempt to scare him and divert him from his destiny, but he failed. I believe Nehemiah's incredible success was dependent on his ability to master fear and refusal to let go of his destiny.

I have already mentioned my deliverance from fear. Part of that was my decision to say: "Enough is enough! Fear, from now on I am your master!" The bottom line is this: the only power the devil has over your life is the power you give him.

Increase your prayer levels

One of the other things I have learned is that, as I follow God and He leads me into new situations and higher levels of service and responsibility, there are 'different devils for different levels'. Since purchasing the Dream Centre, I have experienced different levels and methods of attack than I had experienced before, and some that I already had, but to a greater degree. Please understand that my aim here is not to glorify the devil, but to help us identify and resist his attacks. We must remember, within all this, that he is a defeated foe. We simply have to walk in trust, working out that already-won victory in our daily lives.

Our response to all this means that we have to, by absolute necessity, become men and women of prayer. God showed me a couple of years ago that, as good as I felt it was at the time, my prayer life was inadequate for what I was dealing with. I needed to step it up and mix it in with fasting. There will be times and seasons when we need to step it up. Maybe you're going through one of those seasons right now and are beginning to realise that what appeared to be sufficient prayer in the past is not enough to get you through what you're facing now. If so, step it up!

Be strong and courageous

In virtually every area of national life, and particularly sport, politics and business, you have to pity the people who follow a legend. They normally fail simply because no one, no matter how amazing, can compete with the previous incumbent's record. Can you imagine being the man who followed after Moses? Joshua was that man. He drew the short straw, and unsurprisingly he was a little fearful about taking up the role of leading the rebellious children of Israel into a land full of giant people and giant cities! God's words must have encouraged him:

"Have I not commanded you? Be strong and courageous. Do not be afraid; do not be discouraged, for the Lord your God will be with you wherever you go" (Joshua 1:9).

It takes great courage to lead, but we also need to be strong. Many Western Christians are casual about the battle we are facing, but Paul was very clear:

> *Be strong in the Lord and in his mighty power. Put on all of God's armour so that you will be able to stand firm against all strategies of the devil. For we are not fighting against flesh-and-blood enemies, but against evil rulers and authorities of the unseen world, against mighty powers in this dark world, and against evil spirits in the heavenly places* (Ephesians 6:10-12, NLT).

I refuse to allow the fears I face to restrict my trust in God, or to become limitations and boundaries. I have asked God to strengthen me for these battles. I have realised in recent years how much the enemy can attack my thought life and create worry, anxiety, fears and speculations, so I have had to make a choice that I won't entertain any thought that is not from Him. I make every attempt to guard my heart and my mind. I've particularly asked Him to give me a strong mind that has the ability to resist the enemy until he flees from me.

I try to be prayerfully on the alert for enemy attacks. I keep a close eye on my radar and refuse to allow any thoughts that might undermine my trust in God to land. I find this a useful declaration to make, straight from God's word:

"Surely the righteous will never be shaken; they will be remembered for ever. They will have no fear of bad news; their hearts are steadfast, trusting in the Lord. Their hearts are secure, they will have no fear; in the end they will look in triumph on their foes" (Psalm 112:6-8).

I've made the choice that, as a child of God, I will no longer be a slave to fear. I will no longer allow it to rule me and, like David, I will declare my trust in Him whenever I feel fearful:

"When I am afraid, I put my trust in you. In God, whose word I praise —
in God I trust and am not afraid. What can mere mortals do to me?"
(Psalm 56:3-4).

When we choose to trust God and reject fear, we live in peace.

Do it afraid!
I love the story of Elisabeth Elliot, whose husband Jim was killed along
with four other missionaries in Ecuador, as I shared earlier. She said
that at one time her life was completely controlled by fear. Every time
she started to step out and minister, fear stopped her. Then a friend
told her something that set her free: "Why don't you do it afraid?"

Elisabeth listened and took that advice. Together with Rachel
Saint, the sister of one of the murdered missionaries, she went on to
evangelise the Indian tribes of Ecuador, including the very people who
had killed their loved ones.[lxx]

Sometimes we have to face down fear. We have to look it right
in the face. We often think we should wait until we are no longer
afraid before we do something, but if we did that we would probably
accomplish very little for God, for others, or even for ourselves. Both
Abram and Joshua had to step out in faith and do what He had
commanded them to do, even though they were afraid.

Fear shipwrecks faith and destroys trust in God. I wonder how
many times the enemy of our souls has used fear to stop people
trusting God. John Wimber said that, 'Faith is spelt 'R-I-S-K'. [lxxi] Fear
foils risk, so do it afraid!

Fear of growing older
I wonder how you feel about getting older. When you're young you
think life will last forever, and once you're middle-aged you realise
how quickly time flies! We simply have to accept that ageing is part of
God's plan for our lives and thank Him for every breath we have.

Sadly, many come to regard old age as something to be
dreaded. I doubt that anyone wants to be old and unable to do some
of the things they used to be able to do easily. Nobody wants to
become dependent on others, face health challenges or experience

loneliness as children scatter across the world and family members and friends pass on.

I've realised more and more that God keeps us breathing for a reason. He has a plan and a purpose for us, and in our latter years we must be grateful for that life and breath that has sadly eluded others. While enjoying and choosing to be content in our latter years, we must make sure that we continue to use our spiritual gifts, natural abilities, personalities and experiences to serve others and glorify God.

I'm delighted that we have so many senior people serving in our church. In fact, our outreach ministries would probably collapse without their energy, enthusiasm, experience and gifts, and I know that they value the opportunity. It makes them come alive!

I love what CS Lewis said: *"The great thing is to be found at one's post as a child of God, living each day as though it were our last, but planning as though our world might last a hundred years."*[lxxii]

I also believe we should focus on heaven. The older we get, the closer we come to the glorious eternity where there will be no more aches, pains, sickness, suffering or death. We can trust that God has prepared a wonderful place for us.

As I've had the privilege of talking to people during their final hours on earth, I've sometimes suggested that if we imagine the world on the best possible day – maybe a favourite holiday place – the sun is always shining and there isn't a cloud in the sky. No anxieties or worries fill that moment, and we almost wish we could freeze time and stay there in that moment forever. I tell them that is what heaven will be like, only a million times better. We can trust the God who created this incredible universe that heaven will be completely off the scale.

For us this is the end of all the stories...But for them it was only the beginning of the real story. All their life in this world...had only been the cover and the title page: now at last they were beginning Chapter One of the Great Story which no one on earth has read: which goes on for ever: in which every chapter is better than the one before (CS Lewis).[lxxiii]

Eternity is going to be absolutely amazing, so we must make sure that we live the life God has given us to the full, knowing that there is no rerun. We must live out the purposes for which God has put us on earth so we can hear those famous words: *"Well done, good and faithful servant"* (see Matthew 25:23).

This life is our preparation for eternity. One day, each of us will stand before God to give account of our lives and what we did with what He gave us. If we know Jesus Christ as Lord, *"an inheritance that can never perish, spoil or fade is kept in heaven for [us]"* (see 1 Peter 1:4).

Imagine

Why not make the choice today that you will face any fears you have head on? Enough is enough! You will not be plagued by or restricted by them one second longer. You will, by trusting God, and with His help, master your fears. Trust me, God will help you do this. You must choose to be a slave to fear no longer. After all, you are a child of God! Why don't you swap fear for faith? Then you will begin to move into all that God has planned for you.

Why don't we use our imaginations more? Children have vivid imaginations and are always dreaming and playing make-believe games. Down the centuries, our world has been changed forever by the imaginations of its inhabitants. Christopher Columbus imagined far-off shores, while Martin Luther King imagined a world where black and white cohabited peacefully. Nelson Mandela imagined a free South Africa. Alexander Graham Bell imagined a time when people could communicate in different locations via a cable. Walt Disney imagined a magical kingdom. The list goes on...

Imagine what you would attempt if you weren't fearful and knew you couldn't fail. Imagine if you chose to ignore your fears and 'do it afraid' by stepping out for God. Imagine what He could do with your life.

"Our greatest fear should not be of failure but of succeeding at things in life that don't really matter" (DL Moody).[lxxiv]

Chapter 16

With your money

It was early Sunday morning on the day of our church's gift day in 1998. We were hoping to raise thousands of pounds for the refurbishment of the shopping centre in Crewe that we had purchased and were slowly converting into a church centre. I was praying and considering my message when I was interrupted by God, who said: "Simon, I want you and Julia to be an example to the congregation of sacrificial giving. I do not want the congregation to think that you are asking them to make a sacrifice that you are unwilling to make yourselves. I want you to donate £5,000 to the church and show them the cheque."

Julia and I had always been generous to the church and in building God's kingdom. We gave above and beyond what we believe to be the biblical mandate of ten percent, and supported other organisations and individuals, but this was a further challenge to obey God. We had recently sold our home and had £19,000 left to put down a deposit on our first home. We were acutely aware that prices were rising quickly. To be honest, we were already struggling to get together enough deposit on a home big enough for our family of seven.

You can only imagine the reaction from Julia when I took her a cup of tea and shared this word with her! Let's just say that she wasn't immediately in agreement. She wasn't particularly happy when I went ahead with it publicly at church that morning, but she trusted me and, more importantly, she trusted God. Our congregation was inspired and gave thousands of pounds that day sacrificially. Praise God!

However, this left us with a much smaller deposit to put down on a house. We looked for several months but found ourselves quite limited by what we could afford. Nevertheless, God is faithful. He led us to a lovely four-bedroomed home in a cul-de-sac that we had completely missed, and we were able to haggle a price we could literally just afford. If the owner had wanted another five pounds we wouldn't have been able to pay it. Isn't God good? He is trustworthy and true, and will always honour us when we trust Him with our worldly possessions and money.

It took me several years to really trust God with my money, and at times I have been tempted to sort things out for myself, particularly when I unwisely allowed us to get into debt as a family. I always wanted the best for my children and hated them missing out simply because I was at college, and then later when planting a church on a low income. However, I have always erred on the side of trusting God rather than money.

The biggest challenge

"Trust in the Lord with all your heart and lean not on your own understanding; in all your ways submit to him, and he will make your paths straight" (Proverbs 3:5-6).

Having taught us to rely on God, Solomon immediately identifies the biggest challenge for those who have committed to live out his challenge. It comes in the verses immediately following our theme verses:

"Do not be wise in your own eyes; fear the Lord and shun evil. This will bring health to your body and nourishment to your bones. Honour the Lord with your wealth, with the first fruits of all your crops; then your barns will be filled to overflowing, and your vats will brim over with new wine" (Proverbs 3:7-10).

Solomon links the verses together, and it is clear that wholehearted trust most definitely includes the area of trusting God with our money and honouring Him with our first fruits (ten percent). I was so tempted to leave this bit out of the book, but the link is unavoidable, I'm afraid. Jesus, who taught more on money than on any other single subject, said:

'Do not store up for yourselves treasures on earth, where moths and vermin destroy, and where thieves break in and steal. But store up for yourselves treasures in heaven, where moths and vermin do not

destroy, and where thieves do not break in and steal. For where your treasure is, there your heart will be also' (Matthew 6:19-21).

He also said:

"'No one can serve two masters. Either you will hate the one and love the other, or you will be devoted to the one and despise the other. You cannot serve both God and Money'" (Matthew 6:24).

While we don't have space for an in-depth study on either passage, I think it's clear from Jesus' teaching that He expects us to be good stewards of what He has given us, and that we must not allow money to rule us. We must master our money and use it wisely. He also taught that:

"'Whoever can be trusted with very little can also be trusted with much, and whoever is dishonest with very little will also be dishonest with much. So if you have not been trustworthy in handling worldly wealth, who will trust you with true riches?'" (Luke 16:10-11).

Being faithful with our money gives a good indication that we can handle true spiritual riches. God watches what we spend our money on, how we pay our bills and organise our priorities, and the way we produce and handle our money. He then decides whether we are faithful and can be trusted with spiritual riches.

I sense once again that God would encourage us by saying this: if you trusted me more today with your money, imagine what I would trust you with tomorrow.

Do you trust God with your money?

In all my years as a Christian and a pastor, this area has represented the biggest challenge for me and the many believers I have spent time with. Trusting God with all our hearts involves *everything* in *every* area of our lives. This includes our worldly wealth.

If you can't trust God with your money, you'll struggle to trust Him in other areas of your life. I'm almost tempted to repeat that, such is its importance! Consider your life for one moment and ask yourself if this is true.

Wrong question!
To be honest, this question is completely the wrong way around. To put it correctly: can God trust us to be good stewards of His money?

Why do I say this? Because the Bible clearly teaches that everything we have is already His:

"The earth is the Lord's, and everything in it..." (Psalm 24:1; 1 Corinthians 10:26).

You might reply: "But I've studied and worked hard for my money over the years" or "I'm the one who has built this business". However, I would suggest that the gifts and abilities you have used to get it were given by God, as were the doors that opened and the opportunities that arose to create your wealth. Everything came from God. Absolutely everything.

"You may say to yourself, 'My power and the strength of my hands have produced this wealth for me.' But remember the Lord your God, for it is he who gives you the ability to produce wealth, and so confirms his covenant, which he swore to your ancestors, as it is today" (Deuteronomy 8:17-18).

Maybe as you read those words you will receive a fresh perspective on everything you have. As Jentezen Franklin put it:

"God owns all the donuts. If he wants to, he can take all the donuts off your plate and just walk away. But he's a good God and he keeps blessing you and blessing you."[lxxv]

Tithing

I'm not going to talk about the tithe (ten per cent) very much, except to mention five brief things:

- I absolutely believe in tithing, and I've practised it all my adult life, even during periods when we had little or no money. God has always blessed us and provided during these times.
- Tithing is a massive trust challenge. If you say that you trust God and can afford to (some would say you can't afford not to!) but don't tithe your money when you receive it, the question has to be asked: where does your trust lie? In God or in your bank account?
- I don't believe I'm being generous when I give ten percent as it's the biblical minimum. In some respects, it's a simple test of our faith. Do we trust Him enough to put aside the first ten percent of our income and give it to our local church to help build His Kingdom?
- When I tithe, I'm submitting to God and coming under His spiritual authority. For some reason, God chose to record the story I mentioned earlier of when Abraham gave ten percent of everything he had to Melchizedek as an acknowledgement that he was a higher spiritual authority in Abraham's life. I find it a wonderful thing to submit to God and honour Him with my first fruits. I love Him, so why wouldn't I want to honour Him in this way?
- We could argue all day about the tithe being under the Old Covenant and not under the New Covenant. However, this isn't really a valid argument as the Early Church believers gave pretty much everything they had. No one was in need. I believe the New Testament expectation is for us to be even more generous and joyful as we give.

I would never force anyone to pay their tithe, but I always encourage people to reconsider if they are reluctant. There is a powerful concept of love, submission and trust at work here. Why would you not want to show your love for God by trusting Him with your money and bringing your first fruits to Him every month? Anyway, it's your call and your choice.

It's a big challenge
We live in difficult days, and money is tight for many. So what should our response be?

Be good stewards
Ultimately, everything we have comes from God, including our time, money, homes, gifts and abilities. We have a massive responsibility to be good stewards and to use what we have been given to provide for ourselves and our families, but also to bless others and provide for His Kingdom.

Jesus talked a lot about stewardship and managing the resources we have been given well. He warned against hoarding and also reminded us that the Master expects a return on His investment. The stewardship of our money always reveals our true priorities. Let's make sure we are good stewards of everything He has given us.

Be as generous as possible
The Pharisees tithed religiously, but no one would say they had generous spirits. They often did it to be seen.

Jesus commended the widow for quietly and discreetly giving her two small coins (see Mark 12:41-44), which was everything she had, rather than the Pharisees, who made a big song and dance about their minimal giving. The widow demonstrated a deep trust in God. She gave everything she had out of generosity, not knowing where her next meal was coming from.

Generosity normally costs us something. God calls us to be generous in every way, and this involves personal sacrifice. Generosity isn't related to your wealth or income. The Christians in Macedonia clearly caught God's heart on this:

In the midst of a very severe trial, their overflowing joy and their extreme poverty welled up in rich generosity. For I testify that they gave as much as they were able, and even beyond their ability.

Entirely on their own, they urgently pleaded with us for the privilege of sharing in this service to the Lord's people (2 Corinthians 8:2-4).

God promises to provide for the generous:

Now he who supplies seed to the sower and bread for food will also supply and increase your store of seed and will enlarge the harvest of your righteousness. You will be enriched in every way so that you can be generous on every occasion, and through us your generosity will result in thanksgiving to God (2 Corinthians 9:10-11).

This is a heart matter, but let's make it our aim to be as generous as we can be towards God and others. We are never more like God than when we are being generous.

Supporting our churches
First and foremost, let's make sure we support the local church generously. According to my Bible, tithes should primarily go into His storehouse, which is the church you attend. Other giving, such as supporting missions work, charitable work, Christian TV, food banks, individuals and family members, should be in addition to our tithes.

Most churches today are struggling because they are massively underfunded. Recent statistics suggest that:

- Only seven percent of Christians tithe
- Between twenty-five and fifty percent give nothing at all
- Two-thirds churches are really struggling financially[lxxvi]

Most pastors, myself included, find it difficult to preach about money. People don't want to hear about it, and the accusation is sometimes made that "all the pastor talks about is money" (not without good reason, according to the stats!).

Can I encourage you to really support and provide generously for the ministry of your local church? You wouldn't expect to go to watch a movie and put your small change into the cashier's hand for your ticket. Remember that you and your family receive much more at your local church, and it costs money to run. Sadly, that is how some view the offering. Rather than planning ahead to give, they just throw in some loose change. That wouldn't get you into a movie and it shouldn't be our attitude considering the much greater blessings we receive at our local churches, and the blessing of God on our lives.

Provide for the poor and needy

In addition to giving to the churches we attend, we should try to create enough margin in our finances so we can look after the poor, oppressed and disadvantaged in society. There is a clear biblical mandate for this throughout the Bible, and it's an amazing opportunity to share God's love with struggling and hurting people.

Why don't we give generously to God?

There are many reasons why people don't give. Perhaps they don't believe their church needs the money, or they never got around to it, or they're very careful with their money because their parents never had any and they've decided to make sure that never happens again. Sometimes it's simply because they feel they can't afford it right now. Their budget just doesn't allow for it.

That aside, I believe the biggest reason is that most of us are genuinely fearful of giving. The day Julia and I gave that money towards our building fund, we both felt a bit fearful. We had five young children to feed and no home of our own. It would have been easy to say: "We can't afford it" or "What if there isn't enough money to put down as a deposit?" or "What if we get an unexpected bill?" All of these were genuine concerns.

Fear destroys generosity, and we know where it comes from. On the other hand, faith to be generous comes from our incredibly generous Father. We must make the decision to go beyond our fears and trust God for everything we need. He doesn't want our generosity to be restricted by fear.

We have a choice to trust Him financially and experience the joy of participating in His plans and purposes on earth, or to trust in our own ability to earn money and live with the constant anxiety of not having enough to get by. One of the great dangers of the latter choice is that you miss the opportunity to be involved in something amazing that God wants to do for or through you.

At some point, I can guarantee that the opportunity will arise to give way beyond what you've ever given before. Fear will say: "No way, because..." And faith will say "Come on, trust God and do it!" At this point, you get a choice as to whether to live a fuller or lesser life. The question is, will you really trust in the Lord with all your heart, or will you carry on as you are? I pray that you will trust Him. Imagine what God could do in your life if you trusted Him more today.

Why does God want us to give?

Being generous is good for us
God wants us to be the people He created us to be: people who are beautifully whole, content, generous and those who bless others. He wants to free us from the attitudes that distort and rob us of our identity.

Proverbs 11:24-25 (MSG) says: *"The world of the generous gets larger and larger; the world of the stingy gets smaller and smaller. The one who blesses others is abundantly blessed; those who help others are helped."*

We can experience the joy of giving
Blessing and providing for other people is such fun! Paul records Jesus' statement that: *"It is more blessed to give than to receive"* (Acts 20:35). Every time I'm generous I get such a buzz from it, and whenever I'm mean I feel horrible inside. I choose generosity over meanness and joy over misery every time.

We get to be countercultural
So many people live lives that revolve around 'me, me, me', and what they need, want and desire, but we are called to be different. God wants us to live expansive, generous lives that bless others, and to be a message from Him to the people around us. How can these people experience His amazing generosity? Through *our* generosity.

Obedience always brings blessing

God commands us to give generously, and to do so out of love and obedience to Him. The Bible is full of promises about generosity. Here are a couple:

"Give, and it will be given to you. A good measure, pressed down, shaken together and running over, will be poured into your lap. For with the measure you use, it will be measured to you" (Luke 6:38).

Remember this: whoever sows sparingly will also reap sparingly, and whoever sows generously will also reap generously. Each of you should give what you have decided in your heart to give, not reluctantly or under compulsion, for God loves a cheerful giver. And God is able to bless you abundantly, so that in all things at all times, having all that you need, you will abound in every good work (2 Corinthians 9:6-8).

The fact is, God wants to partner with us so we can be even more generous. Now there's a thought!

How can you begin to trust God more with your money?

Make the choice to trust Him with all your heart in the area of personal finance, and start reorganising your money so you're able to give more. It's my belief that God is looking for habitual, instinctive, generous and joyful givers. How can we do this?

- Create a budget to bring order to your spending, making space so you are free to be generous. There are lots of online tools to help you organise your budget.
- Create an emergency fund. Set aside £500 as soon as you can so you have money for emergencies and don't have to wreck your budget or debt cancellation plan to buy a new washing machine or repair the car.
- Get out of debt as soon as you can. One of the reasons so many Christians struggle to give freely and generously is that they have allowed themselves to amass extensive debt. Please don't feel condemned if this is you. Seek some help and advice

as soon as you can. Christians Against Poverty (capuk.org) is a brilliant Christian charity that has helped many people get out of debt and reorganise their budgets. Getting out of debt will be a huge breakthrough, and then you'll have the freedom to be really generous. Solomon taught that: *"The rich rule over the poor, and the borrower is slave to the lender"* (Proverbs 22:7). While it's OK to borrow for necessities, I believe we should always pay for luxuries. If possible, pay cash or don't buy it at all.

- Start to give to God. The first port of call is His Church. The 'storehouse' mentioned in the Bible is the Church. Even if you have very little — maybe you're a student, pensioner, unemployed or in debt — God will honour you. Start with a percentage in mind and give regularly. Try to hit ten percent as soon as you can. You will be amazed at what God does in response to your giving.

- Become an even more generous giver. For those of you who already give ten percent, how about being even more generous? Consider increasing your 'tithe'. Give extravagantly! Actively look for opportunities to provide for the Kingdom of God and His people.

Are you ready to bless others?

God often presents us with openings to bless others financially. Julia and I love to do this. It's the heart of God, and these opportunities will come if we have open ears.

When I was at Bible college, we were doing our weekly shopping at a discount food store with what little money we had. The food there was always really cheap, and often horrible! Still, it was all we could afford during that season. I saw a fellow student across the aisle and God instantly whispered in my ear that I should give him the twenty pounds in my pocket. That was pretty much all we had to spend on shopping for our large family. After a brief 'discussion' with God, I gave the guy the money. Barely pausing to say thank you, he dashed out of the store.

A few days later, he told me he had been praying that God would provide him with some cash to drive to Scotland for an important family reunion later that day. Apparently, the whole family was gathering for the first time in years and several members had not spoken for a long time. He was able to bring about a wonderful reconciliation. Isn't God good? Julia and I were so blessed when we discovered we had been used by God to facilitate that opportunity.

Just last year, Julia and I attended a conference at a hotel in Hull. Over breakfast, I noticed that one of the waitresses was really angry and aggressive. Initially, I was offended by her behaviour, but then I felt God prompt me to bless her by giving her a big tip, and to show her some appreciation for her hard work. She was so surprised and grateful when I spoke to her. I had several conversations with her during the remainder of the conference and was able to share my faith with her. This resulted in her agreeing to attend the church hosting the conference the following Sunday.

I've learned that when we have generous hearts, stay open to the Holy Spirit and are willing to act in simple obedience, God will use us to bless other people's lives with what He has already given us. It is God's heart for us to trust Him and be good stewards of all He has blessed us with.

Trust God by giving generously

Can I encourage you to give generously and habitually? You may not agree with tithing, but make a decision to be a generous follower of Jesus.

Julia and I have discovered that you cannot out-give God. There have been times when we have struggled, but on many other occasions He has blessed us suddenly and way beyond our expectations. He is so good!

Generous people

God has called us all to be generous people. I have met so many mean and tight-fisted people, and the particularly sad thing is that some of them are Christians. God blesses us to be a blessing to others. He certainly doesn't bless us to be mean. I believe God often trusts those He knows to be generous with worldly riches. He created us in His image and His desire is that we lead lives that reflect the heart of the kind and generous Father He truly is. He is looking for people He can trust to be generous, and His promise is this:

"Give, and you will receive. Your gift will return to you in full—pressed down, shaken together to make room for more, running over, and poured into your lap. The amount you give will determine the amount you get back" (Luke 6:38, NLT).

Imagine

The rich young ruler desired to completely trust Christ and follow him (see Luke 18:18-23). He was clearly a very capable man. I suspect he was rich because he was smart, gifted and able to produce income, yet he was fearful and failed to trust God. I wonder what God would have trusted this young man with had he been willing to trust Him with his money. Imagine what God would trust you with tomorrow if you trusted Him more today!

What do you need to do in order to be more generous towards God and His people? Is it time to face down your fears about not having enough money and choose instead to have faith in God as your provider?

Do you need to create a budget, clear your debts, create an emergency fund or begin to save? What can you do financially to support the ministry of your local church? Could you increase your giving or use your business to bless the ministry of the church financially?

We're called to be good stewards of all that God has given us. What are you doing with everything He has blessed you with? Consider your time, gifts, abilities, money, home and experience. Don't forget to watch and listen for opportunities to bless those around you.

Chapter 17

From now on

Learning to trust God is a journey we are all on, and God deliberately allows each of us to experience it in different ways in order for our faith and trust to grow. My second work promotion involved moving to a small town in Cambridgeshire. I was so excited by another promotion and the opportunity to experience a new place; however, I soon discovered that the demands of my new job would supersede anything I had experienced before, and I was a grafter.

My new boss was a good guy but a total workaholic who lived to work rather than working to live. Life became very challenging and incredibly lonely for me. I initially lived by myself in a one-bedroomed flat and spent most evenings and weekends on my own for more than a year, which wasn't something a young man in his early twenties is used to, or, in my opinion, built for. I remember walking around the town centre in the evenings, desperately looking for someone to talk to.

God allowed the normal support structures of family and friends to be removed for a season so he could teach me to completely depend on Him. At one point I rented a house very cheaply, and part of the deal was that I looked after the owners' two small dogs. I can still picture the fields I exercised the dogs in, and I distinctly remember the long conversations I had with God.

It was a desperately lonely but precious season of my life. Father God became my closest companion and confidant. He helped me through all the desperately isolated times and pressure periods at work. Most importantly, He taught me to rely solely on Him. It was in this town that God called me to full-time ministry.

"O my people, trust in him at all times. Pour out your heart to him, for God is our refuge" (Psalms 62:8, NLT).

During this season of my life, I learned to talk to God and pour out my heart to him, especially when my boss was giving me a really hard time. I got better at listening to Him and relying on His Word to speak into my situation. This was pre-internet, mobile phones and social media, and landline charges were high. Apart from a weekly call to my mum, there was really no one else to talk to. Sadly, it took me a long time to find a church and pastor to link up with. God undoubtedly allows us to face challenging seasons in order to build trust into our lives. He wants us to depend on Him.

Make a choice
Whatever your current situation, I want to encourage you to really learn to trust God from now on. You may be a student, a newlywed, middle-aged, retired or unemployed. You may be recently bereaved and at a loss as to what to do next, or a single parent with the massively challenging role of bringing up children while holding down a job, given little or no support. Whatever your context, make a choice (declare it out loud if necessary!) that you will depend on him wholeheartedly, starting today.

The future might appear daunting, but you can trust Him with all your heart. Don't try to work it all out; simply trust Him.

"Never be afraid to trust an unknown future to a known God" (Corrie ten Boom).[lxxvii]

The amazing thing is that God will take us at our word as we make the choice to trust Him. He will help us and keep us on track. I love the way *The Message* translates the following passage. What a great challenge followed by a fantastic promise:

"Trust God from the bottom of your heart; don't try to figure out everything on your own. Listen for God's voice in everything you do, everywhere you go; he's the one who will keep you on track. Don't assume that you know it all. Run to God! Run from evil! Your body will glow with health, your very bones will vibrate with life! (Proverbs 3:5-8, MSG).

However, He also expects us to play our part. Trust is a verb, an action, a doing word. Trust isn't something I can do for you, or vice versa. We have to do it *by* ourselves, *for* ourselves. Trust is a choice we have to make, even when we don't feel like it. I don't always feel like going to the gym for a workout, but I choose to do so. In the same way, I don't allow my feelings dictate whether I trust or not. I just have to do it, and so do you.

So what can we do to make sure that we stay on track?

Stay close to God

This is absolutely critical, and without doing so we will undoubtedly sway from the path. Remember our friend Christian from *The Pilgrim's Progress*? Staying close to God doesn't mean simply praying and reading our Bibles, but rather involving Him in every aspect of our lives. He wants to be involved in every aspect of our lives from our waking to our sleeping. He desires to be involved with our working, resting, playing, thinking, speaking, laughing, crying, hoping and dreaming. Let's walk and talk with Him throughout our daily lives.

Make time for fellowship

If we're going to stay on track, we must have regular fellowship with other Christians. We were created for relationship, and there are so many benefits in spending time with God's people. One of the trends today, particularly in Western Christianity, is to attend church less regularly. Many pastors are concerned about this as fellowship with other believers is crucial.

If your church has small groups that meet midweek in people's homes, join one! There you will be able to share with others who are on a similar journey. In that safe place, you can give and receive love, support, encouragement, comfort, help and prayers, while also using the specific gifts God has given you to minister into other people's lives. We need one another on this journey through life. We were not created to be solitary Christians.

Obey God promptly

We've already made the choice to let Him lead our lives, but that's only the beginning. We must learn to obey Him *promptly*. This is a recognition that He knows best. When we disobey, we are stating emphatically that we know better! Obedience brings blessing and the favour of God on our lives. Why would we choose any other course of action?

Don't let the world mould you

We are continually warned in the Bible about the impact the world in which we live can have on us. Paul warned the Roman believers not to let the world mould them or influence their thinking, and John wrote:

> *Do not love the world or anything in the world. If anyone loves the world, love for the Father is not in them. For everything in the world—the lust of the flesh, the lust of the eyes, and the pride of life—comes not from the Father but from the world. The world and its desires pass away, but whoever does the will of God lives for ever* (1 John 2:15-17).

It's so easy for us to be taken in by the desires of the world and all its trappings. We should remember that we brought nothing into it and we can take nothing with us when we die. There are so many amazing experiences to be gained from what is now a global community, but if we aren't careful we can be drawn away. Not only can we be distracted from the right path, but I've seen people lose their faith completely, and often it starts with something small.

Don't keep looking back

"Look straight ahead, and fix your eyes on what lies before you. Mark out a straight path for your feet; stay on the safe path. Don't get sidetracked; keep your feet from following evil" (Proverbs 4:25-27, NLT).

The story of Lot's wife reminds us that we should never look back. If we allow him to, the enemy will use the past to rob us off our future. We simply mustn't let him make us dwell on the past. I guess all of us have memories we would rather not revisit; things that cause us pain or shame; bad choices, unwise decisions, regrets and sinful behaviour.

Providing that we have asked forgiveness and given it to God, there is no need to keep revisiting any of these.

God wants us to trust Him that Jesus dealt with all that stuff, once and for all, on the cross. He is more concerned that we trust Him from now on as He takes us along the right paths. He has a great plan for your life, so don't allow the enemy to spoil it. Look forward, not back!

Don't get side-tracked

Our youngest son, Ashley, used to get side-tracked all the time. We would send him upstairs to fetch something, and ten minutes later there would be no sign of him. He would get distracted by his toys, a book or a video game. He was so easily distracted from the task in hand.

If we're going to trust God from now on, we have to make sure that we allow nothing to distract us from all that He has for us. We must stay away from things that are clearly evil, but also take care not to get sucked into seemingly attractive and perhaps even godly causes that take us onto a different path from the ones we set out on. I've realised that sometimes good can be the enemy of the best!

It does us no harm to check every now and then that we are still on the right path. If you stay on your current path, will it lead where you want to go or where you sense God is calling you?

"Give careful thought to the paths for your feet and be steadfast in all your ways" (Proverbs 4:26).

Don't quit!

The road can be very rough and steep at times, and most of us have felt the temptation to quit. I certainly have on many occasions. The devil will often tempt people to bow out just when they are on the verge of a breakthrough. While he cannot see into the future, he senses destiny and understands calling, and will do his utmost to wreck God's plans. We must understand that the battle is very real, and that we face an experienced foe. However, the One who is in us is greater than the one who is in the world (see 1 John 4:4).

We must make the choice never to quit, and to stay strong in heart, spirit, mind and emotion. Maybe you need to quit thinking about quitting and start really trusting God again! God will help us with this if we you ask Him.

Don't allow success to distract you

Have you noticed that your prayer life drops off when you're comfortable, well-off and don't desperately need anything from God? We can be very fickle at times. Before the children of Israel entered the Promised Land – the land flowing with milk and honey – God warned them not to forget Him. He anticipated that once they had experienced the blessings of Canaan they would no longer rely on Him:

When you have eaten and are satisfied, praise the Lord your God for the good land he has given you. Be careful that you do not forget the Lord your God, failing to observe his commands, his laws and his decrees that I am giving you this day. Otherwise, when you eat and are satisfied, when you build fine houses and settle down, and when your herds and flocks grow large and your silver and gold increase and all you have is multiplied, then your heart will become proud and you will forget the Lord your God, who brought you out of Egypt, out of the land of slavery (Deuteronomy 8:10-14).

This is exactly what happened. They went completely off track. We must also guard against this. Let's trust God deeply at all times, and not just when we need something from Him. That's dishonouring to our amazing God and Father.

Set your heart on things above

Since, then, you have been raised with Christ, set your hearts on things above, where Christ is, seated at the right hand of God. Set your minds on things above, not on earthly things. For you died, and your life is now hidden with Christ in God. When Christ, who is your life, appears, then you also will appear with him in glory (Colossians 3:1-4).

Paul challenged the Colossian believers to keep their focus right. It's easy to get so caught up in the pressing demands of this world and the people around us that we forget that we're 'aliens and strangers'. Heaven is our home. We're just passing through, and our lives should be a reflection of this truth. What do you need to change to refocus your life? What can we trust God to help us with?

Trust Him for new strength every day

"The faithful love of the Lord never ends! His mercies never cease. Great is his faithfulness; his mercies begin afresh each morning" (Lamentations 3:22-23, NLT).

When we trust in God, who is stronger than us, we can draw from His supernatural power every day to handle whatever we are facing with renewed energy and vigour. Every time I read this verse I'm reminded that, when I awake every morning, there is fresh grace, mercy, strength and empowerment to trust and live for Him.

Paul exhorts the Christians in Ephesus, who were facing all kinds of persecution, to:

"...Be strong in the Lord and in his mighty power" (Ephesians 6:10, NLT).

Trusting God enables you to plug into an incredible power source each day. I have discovered that when I come to the end of myself and my personal strength, He fully equips and empowers me for whatever I may face when I trust in Him.

Trust God to enlarge your capacity to trust

If you will let him, God will use your journey and the experiences you have along the way to develop your capacity to trust. Since purchasing the Dream Centre, we have faced so many challenging situations. I have had to develop new levels of trust, especially concerning my health. I have also had to deal with rampant fear and anxiety at times.

Just as divers learn to increase their capacity to breathe underwater for long periods, I have learned to trust God at a much deeper level. He has been my teacher, and He's a great teacher. Don't be too hard on yourself if your trust capacity appears poor. It's probably a lot deeper than you think.

After twenty-plus years of ministry, I have seen pretty much everything there is to see in church life. One of the things I have realised is that the things that panicked and troubled me in the early years of ministry don't even phase me now. That's not bragging in my ability; it has come from the deepening realisation that I can trust God in those situations. I wasn't able to back then, but I have seen over the years that God is faithful. My capacity to trust Him is much larger now than when I first started out on this journey.

Trust God to reciprocate your trust

As a young Christian, I was given the responsibility of running the local Boys' Brigade football team, and some twenty years later I became chaplain at a professional football club. I was once trusted to clean the lanterns and the loos at the boys' camp I attended. These were jobs I hated, but I did them as well as I could nevertheless. A decade later I was leading the very same camp, and a few years after that I was entrusted with leading a much larger camp.

I was trusted to plant a new church, and to purchase and refurbish a seven-thousand-square-foot former shopping centre into a church and community centre. Years later, God called us to relocate and head up the church we now lead in Newcastle, which has purchased a former bingo hall of some thirty-two-thousand square-feet, and has been converting it into a church and community centre that can meet the many needs of the local community.

I could continue, but I'm not writing any of this is to glorify me. God deserves all the glory for His work in and through me. I'm simply a guy who chose to really trust, and I'm incredulous at what, for reasons known only to Him, He has entrusted me with.

Trusting and trustworthy

We have already identified the massive issue around trust in this world, and how completely untrustworthy many people are, but we must also pause to consider our own lives. An aspect of my trusting God is to prove myself trustworthy. Paul challenged the Corinthians with these words:

"Now it is required that those who have been given a trust must prove faithful" (1 Corinthians 4:2).

If I were to ask your boss, workmates, friends or family members, would they describe you as trustworthy? Can you keep a secret? Is your word your bond? Do you always do what you say you will do? Do you turn up on time? Do you deliver the goods? Do you ever lie or tell 'half-truths' to get yourself off the hook or to make yourself look better? When you're given responsibility, can you be trusted to deliver? Do you ever take shortcuts? Do you ever mislead people or exaggerate? If you can't be trusted in any other context, how can God trust you? That's a stark and uncomfortable question!

So far, most of our focus has been on us trusting God deeply and intrinsically, but what if God can't trust you with His plans and purposes? I know that if we trust God like never before, we will live like never before; however, we will miss out massively if God can't trust us to deliver. Maybe it's worth taking a moment to consider what God might entrust you with if He knew He could really trust you.

Does God know that you'll be faithful to the assignment He has given you? That you'll show up, work hard, serve, pray, give, sacrifice and, most importantly, finish the job? God will only trust us with more once we've proved ourselves faithful in the small things. After all, if you can't show up regularly or on time when you're on the rota at church, and often let the team down, why would God trust you to lead a ministry team or a church?

Are you worthy of an even greater entrustment?

When we prove ourselves worthy of His trust, God knows that He can trust us with new and larger responsibilities. He does this because we have proven ourselves trustworthy and faithful; and because we have learned where the power lies and the success comes from (not from us but from Him!). Until you are found to be trustworthy, He won't trust you with much.

Whoever can be trusted with very little can also be trusted with much, and whoever is dishonest with very little will also be dishonest with much. So if you have not been trustworthy in handling worldly wealth, who will trust you with true riches? And if you have not been trustworthy with someone else's property, who will give you property of your own? (Luke 16:10-12).

God is watching you. He's looking to see whether you will trust Him, and whether you can be trusted with true Kingdom riches. When God entrusts us with something, He expects us to look after it, nurture and care for it, show up for it, develop it, and invest our time, talents and money into it. He will expect us to work hard and make sacrifices to make it fruitful and successful. He expects us to pray, seek Him and build it into something that glorifies Him. He expects us to keep going and not to quit when times get tough, which they undoubtedly will at some point.

Those who have been given trust must prove themselves faithful. Have you been faithful to what God has already entrusted you with?

On Sunday 19th October 2014, my friend Peter Byers gave me a promise from God. He said: "God is going to honour your vision...make sure it's a big one!" As he said this, the presence of the Holy Spirit hit us both, and we knew God had spoken. We were both suddenly overwhelmed with tears. Wow! Thank you, awesome Father. For some of us, the biggest boundary is our imagination. God often has a dream for us that is bigger than the ones we have for ourselves. We must make sure that our dreams aren't too small for the greatest Dreamer of all.

Have you asked God what His dream for your life is? It's such a privilege to be alive and to have breath, but what is it that you have specifically been called to be and do? Is there a bigger dream? Is there a higher calling?

American author H. Jackson Brown Jnr wrote: *"Twenty years from now you will be more disappointed by the things that you didn't do than by the ones you did do. So throw off the bowlines. Sail away from the safe harbour. Catch the trade winds in your sails. Explore. Dream. Discover."*[xxviii]

I believe God wants us to embrace the thoughts He has about us, and the plans and purposes He created for us to fulfil before time began.

British evangelist Smith Wigglesworth said: *"There is no limit to what our limitless God will do in response to a limitless faith."*[lxxix]

Delight yourself in the Lord
As we imagine all that God has for us, it's important that we stay grounded and delight ourselves in Him. It should be our chief aim and joy in life to delight ourselves in Him.

"Trust in the Lord and do good; dwell in the land and enjoy safe pasture. Take delight in the Lord, and he will give you the desires of your heart" (Psalm 37:3-4).

I used to drive past Crewe Alexandra's football ground regularly as it was close to our church centre, and every time I drove past I had a growing desire to become involved with the club. I used to say to God: "If they ever need a chaplain, I'd love to fulfil that role", but I didn't think they had one, so I didn't consider it too much. Several months later, the Salvation Army chaplain serving there came and spoke at our church. He just happened to mention over coffee that he was relocating, and that the football club would need a chaplain when he left.

Fast-forward six months, and several interviews later I was installed as the club's new chaplain. As a football nut, I absolutely loved having the opportunity to get to know the players, staff and fans, and to have the privilege of ministering into the lives of so many people there. It was an amazing four to five years prior to coming to Newcastle, and it's one of the things I miss most now (apart from my amazing kids and grandkids of course!).

I have included this in the book because it illustrates that if we trust God with our lives and follow Him as obediently as we can, He will create opportunities that would never otherwise have been possible. I absolutely believe that He created me with a passion for football, and because I trusted and delighted myself in Him, He was able to open that particular door. I also believe that, as my Father, He received great satisfaction from creating that amazing opportunity for me, His son. He loves to bless His children.

One of the things I have discovered in my walk with God is that the more I trust and delight myself in Him and His ways, and allow Him to shape my life and circumstances, the more He has given me the desires of my heart. When we take delight in the Lord, we are making a choice to do the very things that delight Him. Our desire is to please, obey, love and follow Him. I guess it's about putting Him first in all we do and allowing Him to lead. I believe that when we do this God also takes great delight in us.

As a young boy, my father took me to the Christian camp I mentioned earlier on the beautiful island of Anglesey. The views were outstanding, and I loved the camaraderie, sports and teaching. It was everything a teenage boy would enjoy. I attended for years and made many friends. Towards the end of the leader's long ministry, I remember quite clearly standing in the corner of the big marquee talking to him, and I felt God say to me: "Simon, one day you will lead this camp." Fast-forward some twenty-five years and that is precisely what happened.

During the interim years, I served and sacrificed and waited patiently for the opportunity. Another great leader took charge in the meantime, and God eventually gave me the chance to fulfil my dream. Why am I saying this? Because I believe that God plants desires in our hearts, and then He opens the right doors and creates the necessary opportunities.

Just recently, a really exciting opportunity opened up for me to support a young couple who are launching Elim in the US. This is the country I have longed to minister in because of my parentage. Those desires have been nestling there for decades, and it appears God is now bringing them to the fore. I won't be relocating, but I will be supporting those guys as they seek to establish Elim's presence in America.

But you know what? This isn't about me at all. It's about the God who can be trusted with our lives, who seeks to redeem a lost world and who, for some reason, involves us. He alone deserves all the glory. He is amazing, and I know for a fact that anything that has been of any good or value in my life and ministry is because of Him. Thank you, Father.

I wonder what desires God has planted in your heart. I wonder what you have imagined for your life. Maybe you have a dream to start a business, lead a ministry, write a book, study at college, work with orphans, create a cure for a deadly illness, have a family, teach, or reach the poor and needy.

Over the years I've watched people in my congregation grasp this teaching for themselves. I'm reminded of countless people who have decided to trust God more, and who have sought to place their lives, ambitions and dreams in His hands. I've watched people found new ministries, launch businesses, change careers and discover gifts and abilities they never knew that they had. I've seen people take massive leaps of faith and 'do it afraid'! I've seen people in retirement do incredible things for God. It has been truly wonderful to watch what God has done in them and through them in so many multifaceted ways and contexts. He is amazing!

The promise of God is that, if we delight ourselves in Him, He will give us the desires of our hearts. If we build our lives in God, He will build His life in us. If we begin to trust Him like never before, we will live like never before.

"Now to him who is able to do immeasurably more than all we ask or imagine, according to his power that is at work within us, to him be glory in the church and in Christ Jesus throughout all generations, for ever and ever! Amen" (Ephesians 3:20-21).

Imagine

It's clear that God wants us to trust Him so that we are better equipped and stronger as His people, but also because He has planned things for us that He wants to be sure He can trust us with. It's a journey of trust and God doesn't expect us to suddenly become like Moses or Paul. He does want us to get serious though and to stay close to Him, obey Him, remain on the right path and look to Him at all times. If we do that He promises to be with us, help us, lead us and enlarge our capacity to trust.

As we near the end of the book, perhaps now is a good time to reflect and consider the areas God has spoken to you about specifically. Set time aside to review the questions at the end of each chapter. Take some notes, record them in a journal (it's so useful to keep a journal!) and pray through them, asking God to help you to develop your trust in Him.

A final thought
I know there will be people reading who are on a journey of faith, like so many today. Thank you so much for reading my book. The main theme is trusting God and in doing so, discovering the right path in life.

It's so easy to believe that every spiritual path leads to God. This is what you may hear from those who follow other religions. However, it simply isn't true.

"Jesus answered: *'I am the way, truth and the life. No one comes to the Father except through me'* (John 14:6).

Other religions may promise all kinds of wonderful things, but they don't lead us to God. We need to have a relationship with Him that recognises the death and resurrection of Jesus Christ.

Perhaps you have accepted the lie that every spiritual path leads to God. If so, now is a great time to put that right. He loves you so much and longs to be involved in your life. He longs for you to place your trust in Him. My prayer for you is that you truly discover Father God for yourself. You will not be disappointed. You can invite Him into your life right now by praying this simple prayer:

Father God, I bring myself to you today. I don't know everything about you, but I know that I need you in my life. Please forgive me for all the things I've done wrong and wipe the slate of my life clean. I need a new start today. I'm choosing to trust You today and so I gladly surrender my life to you. Take me just as I am, and come and live in me by your Holy Spirit. Amen.

If you've prayed that prayer, you have become a Christian. Welcome to the family of God! The next thing to do is find a lively, Bible-believing church and start attending. Speak to the pastor and tell him what has happened. If you need help with this, please don't hesitate to contact me through the email below and we'll help you find a good church in your area.

God bless you!
Simon

Feedback
I'd love to receive your feedback on the book and even better, a review on Amazon would be fantastic. Let's get the message of trust out there!

Email
If you have any comments or suggestions or have noticed any typos then please email me at: revlawton@gmail.com

Further reading
You can read more of my thoughts at my website/blog: simonlawton.com

Connect
Twitter: simonlawton
Facebook: simonlawton
Instagram: simonlawton

Small group discussion questions

I've provided some questions to use in your small groups that will act as a guide and help to promote discussion within your group. You may wish to discard some of the questions or use your own. I've also added suggestions for prayer or ministry at the end of each section.

Chapter 1: God has a plan for your life

Icebreaker: Most of us had dreams as small children. What was yours?

Take a look at 1 Corinthians 15:10. This is a powerful verse. What do you think Paul was saying here, and how do you think we can live this out? Does anyone have a testimony to share about accepting themselves the way God created them?

It's amazing to realise that *"we are God's handiwork, created in Jesus Christ to do good works, which God prepares in advance for us to do"* (Ephesians 2:10).

- What does this incredible verse say to you?
- What are those good works?
- Are our good works solely what we do at church?
- How do we discover His plan for our lives now?
- What do you think God's priority is for our lives?
- Is it different for each person?

Prayer ministry
Is anyone in the group struggling to trust God right now? Pray for them as you close the meeting and then commit, as a group, to continue praying for them as they walk through the challenges they are facing.

Chapter 2: Trust is the issue

Icebreaker: Can you think of an example of 'fake news'?

Trust levels are at an all-time low in our world today. Nobody seems to trust anyone and fake news is rife. If you're leading the study, give an example from your life of where you've really struggled to trust someone. Why is it so hard to trust someone once they've let you down? What can you do to restore trust in your own mind?

The book mentions a Barna Group survey, which states that only one in five of us live in a way that makes us completely dependent on God. Follow-up research indicated that such dependence usually only emerges in times of crisis or suffering.

- Why is this and how can the situation be remedied?
- How can we trust anyone?
- What stops us trusting God as Proverbs 3:5-6 urges?
- How would you answer a Christian friend who said they were struggling to trust God?
- How do we regain our lost trust in God?

Prayer ministry
As you close, encourage members of your group to have a one-to-one with God and talk to Him about the struggles they have when it comes to trusting Him. Encourage them to bring anything particularly difficult to Him. Round the time off with a covering prayer (or ask someone else to do so), summarising what you have learned together.

Chapter 3: Trust in the Lord

Icebreaker: How do you define trust?

The story of Jim Elliot's life and martyrdom is well known in Christian circles. What do you think he meant when he said: *"He is no fool who gives what he cannot keep to gain what he cannot lose?"*
Did Jesus say anything similar? Take a look at Matthew 10:38-39 and 16:24-27.

- What are the barriers to trusting God?
- Is one of the issues that we don't really know this God we're told to trust?

- Why should we trust Him?
- What are the dangers of not trusting Him completely and in every area?
- If we're not trusting God, who are we trusting?
- In what areas do you struggle to trust God most and why?
- How can we develop a childlike trust in God again?

Prayer ministry

Pray for everyone in the group that they will let go of any experiences that have become barriers to trusting God so they can develop a childlike trust in Him again.

Chapter 4: What does trusting God with all your heart look like?

Icebreaker: What do we mean by our 'heart?' and what does it mean to trust God with all our heart?

Is Abraham a good example of someone who trusted God with all his heart? If so, why? What can we learn from Abraham's journey of trusting God more?

"Against all hope, Abraham in hope believed and became the father of many nations" (Romans 4:18).

Over the years, many people have gained fresh hope from this verse and renewed their trust in God.

- Can anyone testify to standing on this verse in the past and trusting God and seeing a breakthrough?
- What does it mean to have an undivided heart? (See Psalm 86:11-13.)
- If we're honest, we all have areas in which we struggle to trust God. What do you think are the main areas?
- What does wholehearted trust look like? (See chapter for points on this.)

- AW Tozer said: "The essence of surrender is getting out of God's way so that He can do in us what He also wants to do through us." What did he mean by this?

Prayer ministry
Break off into pairs and, if people are willing, ask them to share one area in which they are struggling to trust God. Pray for each other. If someone finds it tough to share, encourage their partner to pray for their trust to increase anyway.

Chapter 5: Trust and obey

Icebreaker: Read Genesis 22:1-18 (ask everyone to read a verse each). Ask a group member to describe how it must have felt for Isaac as Abraham tied him up. If they are willing, ask them to act it out. This could be used as a light-hearted moment at the start of the meeting.

- Abraham trusted and obeyed God. What would you have done?
- What do you think God's purpose was in asking Abraham to sacrifice Isaac?
- AW Tozer said: *"It is not just trust; it is not just obey. It is trust and obey."* Which one is harder to do?
- Can we claim to trust God if we don't obey Him and ignore His commands?
- Why do we always take so long to obey?
- Does anyone have a testimony of a time when God asked them to make an incredible sacrifice, they did so and He blessed them as a result?
- Every time we say no to God we are saying yes to the enemy of our souls. Discuss.
- When we say 'No' to God we are saying... (see the list in this chapter).
- Abraham trusted, obeyed and was willing to sacrifice his only son, the child of promise. Do you think God asks us to make similar sacrifices today? Give examples.

Prayer ministry
If they feel they can, ask group members to share their greatest trust challenge right now. Pray into that as a group or on a one-to-one basis.

Chapter 6: Stop worrying!

Icebreaker: what's the silliest thing you've ever worried about?

Ask someone to read Philippians 4:4-9. Paul identified a problem that so many of us have. Instead of trusting God, we worry. Many of us will spend hours worrying rather than praying.

- What are the main things people worry about today?
- Studies have shown that a high percentage of the calamities we anticipate and endlessly worry about rarely happen. How does worry impact our lives?
- How can we take back control?
- How do you deal with and conquer worry?
- Are there any antidotes?
- How do we rediscover God's peace, which passes all understanding (see Philippians 4:7)?
- God wants us not to worry about anything but to pray about everything! (see Philippians 4:6). Is this possible?
- Is there anything you can do to guarantee that your prayers are answered?
- Hezekiah laid his threatening letter out before the Lord (see 2 Kings 19:14-19) and God delivered him from the Assyrian King. Has anyone in the group ever done this?

Prayer ministry
Pray for anyone who is worried and has lost their peace, and for those who have received threatening letters or emails. You could encourage anyone who has received a threat to bring it with them and pray about it as a group and lay it before the Lord if this is appropriate. Pray together and see God break through.

Chapter 7: Don't lean on your own understanding

Icebreaker: what shapes your world view? Think about the way you consume information and the people who have the greatest influence on you.

There are so many things that influence our understanding, including our world view. Read Romans 1:1-3 in as many different versions as you have available within the group. Paul warned us against adopting worldly thoughts and values in Romans 12:2. Consider what the general world view is on the important issues of life.

- Do you think we are any different as Christians?
- Have we allowed the world to shape us too much? Are we conscious of just how much the world has shaped and continues to shape our opinions and faith?
- What, or who, should be shaping your understanding?
- How do you go about making major decisions?
- How do you respond when something doesn't go your way? Give an example.

Draw up a list together of dos and don'ts that will help group members as they face important decisions and even disappointments.

Prayer ministry

There are so many issues to address in local and national government. Politicians often seem to be led by public opinion. Pray that our leaders won't lean on their own understanding but will be directed by God. Pray that living and leading the people righteously will be important. Pray for wisdom, revelation, integrity and godliness in our leaders. Pray for national and local leaders by name, and pray for your pastor(s) and leaders by name. Pray for anyone in the group who needs prayer.

Chapter 8: In all your ways acknowledge Him

Icebreaker: are you more of a thinker or a doer?

Sometimes we make decisions based on our own knowledge and understanding, then ask God to bless them once we have taken action. It's usually better to ask first – to acknowledge Him – then wait for an answer before proceeding, but often we get it back to front and rush into things that weren't part of His plan for our lives.

- Have you done ever this and regretted it?
- What does it mean to acknowledge God?
- How can we involve Him more in our lives and decisions?
- Hosea 6:3 talks about *"knowing God"* and Paul declared that he wanted to *"know Christ"*. What do you think this means for us?
- What does it mean to *"let Him lead"* (see Proverbs 3:6-7, CEV)?
- How have you 'let Him lead' recently? Give an example.
- How can we seek His will in all we do?
- Can we learn anything from people like David, Saul, Gideon and Moses?

Prayer ministry

Pray for the group – or ask someone else to – asking that each member will really know God and be known by Him. Ask your group members to pray their own prayers giving God permission to lead. Encourage them to ask forgiveness for any areas where previously they have taken control and not allowed God to lead.

Chapter 9: He will make your paths straight

Icebreaker: has anyone in the group ever taken part in an obstacle race like Tough Mudder? How difficult did you find it?

The author mentioned at the beginning of the book how seemingly difficult his path to Bible college was, yet it was clearly the right path.

Can anyone share a testimony of having been on the right path, which was full of obstacles that God later cleared?

Read out these two verses:

"In all your ways know and acknowledge and recognise Him, And He will make your paths straight and smooth [removing obstacles that block your way]" (Proverbs 3:6, AMP).

"Always let him lead you, and he will clear the road for you to follow" (Proverbs 3:6-7, CEV).

- These great promises remind us that once we are on the right path God will make it straight, clearing the obstacles. Can you remember any examples from the Bible of God doing this?
- What can we learn from the likes of Joshua, David, Esther, Daniel, Nehemiah when we face obstacles on what we know is the right path?
- Consider the obstacles these saints came up against. Could you create a list ten things to do when obstacles occur on the right path?
- Some of the obstacles that appear can occur on both the right and the wrong path. How do we know which is which? What should you do if you're not sure?

Prayer ministry
Is anyone in the group facing obstacles on the right path? Remind everyone how God straightened out the paths for the author's daughter in terms of her schooling. Gather around those affected and pray that God would clear the obstacles in their lives.

Chapter 10: Discovering the right path

Icebreaker: have you ever taken the wrong path/road? Did it involve a massive detour? How did you feel? Do you have any funny stories to tell?

Jesus talked about the narrow gate that leads to life and the wide gate that leads to destruction (read Matthew 7:13-14).

- What do you think He meant by this? Did He mean literal destruction?
- Why do so few people follow the narrow path?
- Are there any signs that you might be on the wrong path?
- Give examples of when you have gone through the narrow gate and followed the difficult path.
- What happens when we try to chase after two bunnies or have a foot on both paths?
- Do you think God desires to lead us along the right path or a path of right living... or both?
- How do you discover the right path for your life, and how can you stay on it?
- Have you ever, like the author, been directed to take a new path, or has God redirected you from one seemingly good path to one that is even better?

Prayer ministry

Pray for anyone in the group who is particularly seeking direction in their life right now. Ask God to help them discover exactly the right path for the season of their life they are in.

Chapter 11: Through the dark and difficult days

Icebreaker: what is the best thing that has happened to you in the last few weeks? And the worst?

We all go through dark and difficult days, and sometimes it can feel as though God is distant. It's during these times that we really learn to trust God. Sometimes God is pruning us so that we can become all He has made us to be.

- Has anyone been through a really dark season?
- How did you navigate it, and how did your faith help you?
- Has anyone faced similar spiritual battles to those the author shared? How did you deal with them?
- Do we underestimate the power of the enemy? We have God-given power to resist him, but are we too passive?
- Sometimes it feels as though everything that could go wrong does go wrong. What can we do during these difficult periods? (The book lists at least four options.)
- Has anyone been through times of loss or change of circumstances only to realise that God is actually pruning them?
- How can we encourage ourselves in the Lord during the darkest days (see 1 Samuel 30:6-7)?
- What are the benefits of choosing to trust God?

Prayer ministry
There may be someone in the group who has recently entered a dark season of the soul. Try not to embarrass them, but offer to pray. Encourage them. Love them.

Ask the group members privately to consider how they can bless that person or family. They could send cards, call them, take groceries, provide treats, take the children out and so on.

Chapter 12: When nothing appears to change

Icebreaker: have you ever tried to have a conversation with someone who seems distracted? Did you give up or keep trying?

- Has anyone experienced a time when God appeared to be absent, silent or not answering their prayers?
- What did that feel like? What was praying like?
- What should our response be during those seasons, which we all experience?

- What do you do when nothing appears to be changing?

Ask three people in the group to read out the following passages: Psalm 121:1-4; Philippians 2:14; Habakkuk 3:17-18.

- Is it possible to trust God more than you do today?
- What will the result of this increased trust be?
- One of the dangers of such seasons is that we fail to enjoy the journey because we become so occupied with what God doesn't seem to be doing. How can we guard against this?
- Take a look at the story of the three young Jews in Daniel 3. Do you think you could trust God even if He didn't actually rescue you? (See their reaction in verses 16-18.)

Prayer ministry
Encourage the group as a whole to pray into what they have learned from God's Word. Particularly pray for anyone who is struggling because nothing appears to be changing. Ask for renewed hope, fresh energy and strength to keep going. Share any verses or prophetic words as you pray for them.

Chapter 13: In the major decisions

Icebreaker: what's the hardest decision you've ever had to make?

As we travel through life there will be many major decisions to make, particularly concerning study, career, relationships, homes, money and then finally retirement.

- How do you go about making a major decision? What is the process?
- How can you really trust God in the big decisions?
- God promises to guide us (see Psalm 32:8-10, NLT) and Jesus promised that His sheep would hear and recognise His voice (see John 10:27). How do you hear God's voice? Does God speak to us all differently? How does He speak? How do we know it's Him?

- If you were making a major decision such as marriage or relocating to a new area, how would you come to the final decision? What would you be looking for?
- Are there any dos and don'ts?
- Once you've made your decision, what do you expect next?

Prayer ministry

Is anyone in the group facing a major decision? Make time to pray for them. If you feel comfortable with this, and without asking what the decision is, gather around and encourage people to pray and prophesy over them. Who knows what wonderful confirmations God may bring. Make sure you encourage the individuals concerned to test what has been said. No one should make a decision based on a single prayer or prophetic word.

Chapter 14: With your future

Icebreaker: What would you most love to do if you knew you couldn't fail?

Rusty Rustenbach said: *"You and I live in an age when only a rare minority of individuals desire to spend their lives in pursuit of objectives which are bigger than they are. In our age, for most people, when they die it will be as though they never lived."*

- What does he mean, and how can we make sure our lives are worthwhile?
- Is it possible for each of us to have a dream for our lives, or is that only for the 'superstars'?
- Are there any clues to what God is calling each of us to do?
- What stops us stepping out into our unique destinies?
- What can we do when we know we're called to do something but the doors don't seem to be opening? Can we learn anything from the story of Joseph?
- What did Jesus mean when He talked about being faithful in the small things (see Luke 16:10)?

Prayer ministry

Is there anyone in the group who has a dream you can pray about? Pray for breakthroughs and claim the promises of God. The author attended a group recently at which one lady had long harboured the dream of being a nurse. She had been applying for a place at the local college to train but had been turned down twice. The group prayed for her that night and a miracle happened. She received a place! Prayer works.

Chapter 15: When you feel fearful

Icebreaker: what's your biggest fear?

- Where does fear come from and how do we deal with it?
- What are some of the impacts of fear?
- What impact does it have on our ability to trust God?
- Mark Twain said: *"Courage is resistance to fear, mastery of fear, not absence of fear; it is mastery of fear."* The Bible encourages us to "be strong and courageous" many times, but the devil often causes us to fear. How, through trusting God, can we master fear?
- Does anyone have any examples of how they have learned to master it?
- Do you believe the devil has schemes for each individual life that may include fear? How can we resist him?
- The Bible encourages us to be "strong and courageous" many times. How do we work that out in our daily lives?
- Elisabeth Elliot, whose husband Jim was martyred, lived a life that was controlled by fear until a friend said: "Why don't you do it afraid?" She went on to evangelise the very tribe that murdered her husband. In what areas of your life do you need to "do it afraid"?

Prayer ministry

2 Timothy 1:7 (NLT) says: *"For God has not given us a spirit of fear and timidity, but of power, love, and self-discipline."* Encourage the group to quote this verse whenever they become fearful and to declare: "Oh

God, thank You that You are always with me. Your powerful Holy Spirit lives within me, so whenever I feel fearful I will trust in You." Pray for anyone who has admitted they are struggling with a specific fear.

Chapter 16: With your money

Icebreaker: have you ever been blown away by an incredible act of generosity (financial or otherwise)?

Imagine was written to encourage people to really trust God in every area of their lives. Read Proverbs 3:1-10 together. Of all the subjects Christians loathe talking about, the top one is money. Pastors feel uncomfortable speaking about it and people rarely respond well to teaching on it.

- Why do you think the subject is so taboo?
- What do you think Solomon learned about trusting God?
- Does this apply to our money? Did Jesus say anything similar? (check out Matthew 6:19-21 and Luke 16:10-11). What do you think Jesus was saying here?
- When we talk about 'our money', is it actually ours in the first place? (check out Psalm 24:1; 1 Corinthians 10:26; Deuteronomy 8:17-18).
- It is estimated that only 7% of Christians tithe today. Why is this?
- Does God simply want us to tithe or to be generous? (see Proverbs 11:24-25).
- What impact does generosity have on the people around us?
- Does anyone spring to mind who the group could be generous to? (Use discretion if you know there is someone in the group who needs help.)
- What can you do as a group to bless someone in the group and be generous to them?

Many churches are under-resourced and struggling to make end meets, never mind fulfil their God-given mandates. Find out what your church's main needs are and consider raising your level of giving in order to help. Your pastor will be massively encouraged!

Prayer ministry
Have an open time of prayer reflecting on what you have learned. Pray that each person will reflect the generosity of God. Pray for His provision for your church, and that each person will play their part rather than allowing others to make the sacrifice. Pray for those who are struggling financially that God will provide for them.

Chapter 17: From now on

Icebreaker: Ask members of the group to share what they have learned during this series. Explore what has stood out most and what has changed in terms of their thinking and behaviour since they read the book.

- The chapter contains nine keys to trusting God from now on? What are they? Discuss each one.
- What is the greatest threat when it comes to trusting God?
- What is the greatest threat to God trusting us?
- Discuss 1 Corinthians 4:2 and Luke 16:10-12. How can we prove ourselves worthy of His trust?

Prayer ministry
Ask each person in the group to pray about one thing they've learned from reading the book and to thank God for it. Pray that He will empower every group member to trust Him more. Declare Proverbs 3:5-6 out loud together as a statement of intent.

End notes

[i] Garbo, G.: goodreads.com/quotes/236083-life-would-be-so-wonderful-if-we-only-knew-what.

[ii] Kizziar, T. cited in Chan, F., *Crazy Love: Overwhelmed by a Relentless God* (David C Cook, 2009).

[iii] Smith, J., *How's Your Soul?: Why Everything that Matters Starts with the Inside You* (Nelson Books, 2016).

[iv] Freeguard, G., 'Trust in Time': instituteforgovernment.org.uk/blog/trust-time-trust-civil-servants-has-increased.

[v] Covey, S.M.R., 'How the Best Leaders Build Trust': leadershipnow.com/CoveyOnTrust.html.

[vi] Williams, R., 'The Erosion of Trust': raywilliams.ca/the-erosion-of-trust.

[vii] Walsh, KT., 'Tom Hanks Is Most Trusted American, Obama Far Behind': usnews.com/news/blogs/ken-walshs-washington/2013/05/09/tom-hanks-is-most-trusted-american-obama-far-behind.

[viii] Barna Group, 'Research on How God Transforms Lives Reveals a 10-Stop Journey': barna.com/research/research-on-how-god-transforms-lives-reveals-a-10-stop-journey.

[ix] Christanity.com, Jim Elliot: 'No Fool': christianity.com/church/church-history/church-history-for-kids/jim-elliot-no-fool-11634862.html.

[x] Halloran, K., 'Jim Elliot's Journal Entry With 'He Is No Fool' Quote': kevinhalloran.net/jim-elliot-quote-he-is-no-fool/.

[xi] Definition of 'trust' in English Oxford Living Dictionaries: en.oxforddictionaries.com/definition/us/trust.

[xii] Merriman, S.A., *Religion and the Law in America: An Encyclopedia of Personal Belief and Public Policy* (ABC-CLIO, 2007).

[xiii] Jones, M., 'J.I. Packer on "Cultivating Awe in the Presence of God"': reformation21.org/blog/2015/09/ji-packer-on-cultivating-awe-i.php.

[xiv] Warren, R.: twitter.com/rickwarren/status/399151736256233472?lang=en.

[xv] Encyclopaedia Titanica, 'Music Played on the Titanic': https://www.encyclopedia-titanica.org/godhelp.html.

[xvi] BBC, '"Radio Times" for the State Funeral of Winston Churchill': bbc.co.uk/archive/churchill/11030.shtml?page=txt.

[xvii] Wesley, J., *The Works of the Reverend John Wesley A.M.* (Methodist Book Concern, 1831, p.484).

[xviii] Stanley, C., 'Choosing Faith Over Fear': crosswalk.com/devotionals/in-touch/in-touch-aug-22-2012.html.

[xix] Malm, J., 'You'll Feel Better Once You Give Up': joelmalm.com/2017/03/06/youll-feel-better-once-you-give-up.

[xx] Chappell, P., 'What God Can Do with a Surrendered Life': dailyintheword.org/rooted/what-god-can-do-with-a-surrendered-life.

[xxi] Tozer, A.W., God's *Power for Your Life: How the Holy Spirit Transforms You Through God's Word* (Regal, 2013).

[xxii] Sammis, H., "Trust and Obey": hymnary.org/text/when_we_walk_with_the_lord.

[xxiii] Tozer, A.W., *Experiencing the Presence of God: Teachings from the Book of Hebrews* (ed. James L Snyder: Bethany House, 2011).

[xxiv] Jeremiah, D., *Is This The End?: Signs Of God's Providence In A Disturbing New World* (Thomas Nelson, 2016).

[xxv] Meyer, J., *The Mind Connection: How the Thoughts You Choose Affect Your Mood, Behavior, and Decisions* (Faithwords: 2016).

[xxvi] De Montaigne, M., cited in Goewey, D., '85 Percent of What We Worry About Never Happens': huffingtonpost.com/don-joseph-goewey-/85-of-what-we-worry-about_b_8028368.html.

[xxvii] Goewey, D., '85 Percent of What We Worry About Never Happens': huffingtonpost.com/don-joseph-goewey-/85-of-what-we-worry-about_b_8028368.html.

[xxviii] Definition of "worry" in the Online Etymology Dictionary: etymonline.com/word/worry

[xxix] Meyer, J., *The Power of Simple Prayer: How to Talk to God about Everything* (Hodder & Stoughton, 2010).

[xxx] Lucado, M. *Life to the Full* (Thomas Nelson, 2012).

[xxxi] Murray, A., quoted by Crabtree, C., 'Prayer Time Is Not All About You': crosswalk.com/faith/prayer/prayer-time-is-not-all-about-you.html.

[xxxii] *NIV Study Bible* (Hodder & Stoughton, 1987).

[xxxiii] Schilling, D., 'Knowledge Doubling Every 12 Months, Soon to be Every 12 Hours': industrytap.com/knowledge-doubling-every-12-months-soon-to-be-every-12-hours/3950.

[xxxiv] Human Science, 'Worst Predictions': http://humanscience.wikia.com/wiki/Worst_Predictions.

[xxxv] Tada, J., *The God I Love: A Lifetime of Walking with Jesus* (Zondervan, 2003).

[xxxvi] UCB, 'Change Your Thinking': ucb.co.uk/content/change-your-thinking.

[xxxvii] Mencken, H.L., cited in Rentoul, J., 'There is always a well-known solution to every human problem – neat, plausible, and wrong':

independent.co.uk/voices/comment/for-every-problem-there-is-a-solution-that-is-comprehensive-simple-and-wrong-a6956191.html.

xxxviii Brothers, J., cited by Jana, F.P., 'Monday Quote: Trust Your Hunches': blog.freepeople.com/2013/07/monday-quote-trust-hunches.

xxxix Adams, B.: brainyquote.com/quotes/bryan_adams_437553.

xl Jakes, T.D., '5 T.D. Jakes Quotes That Remind Us to Never Give Up': tdjakes.com/posts/5-t-d-jakes-quotes-that-remind-us-to-never-give-up.

xli Campbell, D., cited by Live, Love, Learn, 'Feeling the Squeeze': pastorkjblog.wordpress.com/2016/03/17/feeling-the-squeeze.

xlii Maxwell, J., 'A Leader's Greatest Things': johnmaxwell.com/blog/a-leaders-greatest-things.

xliii Rickover, H., cited by Perry, W., *Listening to Your Sheep: The Fine Art of Pastoral Diagnosis* (Author House, 2006).

xliv Einstein, A. speaking to Viereck, G., cited by Times Higher Education, 'Is Imagination More Important than Knowledge? Einstein': timeshighereducation.com/features/is-imagination-more-important-than-knowledge-einstein/172613.article#survey-answer.

xlv Packer, J.I., *Knowing God* (Hodder & Stoughton, 1975).

xlvi Gill, J., cited by Sacred Texts: sacred-texts.com/bib/cmt/gill/pro003.htm.

xlvii Peterson, E., *Earth and Altar: The Community of Prayer in a Selfbound Society* (IVP, 1985).

xlviii Wiersbe, W., *Be Skillful (Proverbs): God's Guidebook to Wise Living* (David C. Cook, 2009).

xlix Davidson, F., Stibbs, A.M., Kevan, E.F. (eds), *New Bible Commentary* (Inter-Varsity Fellowship, 1961).

l Best, G., cited by Telegraph Reporters, '16 quotes that define the life and times of George Best': telegraph.co.uk/men/the-filter/16-quotes-that-define-the-life-and-times-of-george-best.

li Lewis, C.S., *The Pilgrim's Regress* (William B Eerdmans, 1992).

lii Fuller, T., "Pisgah Sight" in *Bartlett's Familiar Quotations*, eds. Bartlett, J. and Kaplan, J. (Little, Brown and Company, 1992).

liii Felix, A., cited by Fairchild, M., 'Allyson Felix: Christian Athlete Faith Profile': thoughtco.com/allyson-felix-biography-700345.

liv Hughes, S., *The 7 Laws of Spiritual Success* (CWR, 2002).

lv Hughes, S., *The 7 Laws of Spiritual Success* (CWR, 2002).

lvi Ten Boom, C., *Jesus is Victor* (Kingsway, 1985).

lvii Carlyle, T., cited by Casperson, J.W., *Toward Spiritual Sovereignty: A Secular Bible* (AuthorHouse, 2007).

lviii Graham B., *The Enduring Classics of Billy Graham* (Word Publishing, 2004).

lix Graham, R., cited by UCB, 'God Has a Plan: Trust Him': ucb.co.uk/content/god-has-plan-trust-him.

lx Hughes, S. *The 7 Laws of Spiritual Success* (CWR, 2002).

lxi Peterson, E., *Where Your Treasure Is: Psalms that Summon You from Self to Community* (William B Eerdmans, 1959).

lxii Murray, A., *With Christ in the School of Prayer* (Merchant Books, 2013).

lxiii Torrey, R.A., 'How to Pray': biblebb.com/files/prayer-torrey.htm.

lxiv Abernathy, R., cited by Samuels, C.E., *Blood & Roses* (AuthorHouse, 2014).

lxv Callaway, N., cited by Howe, M., 'Tip Toe if You Must, But Take the Step': linkedin.com/pulse/tip-toe-you-must-take-step-melanie-howe.

lxvi Rustenbach, R., cited by Maxwell, J., 'Success or Significance': success.com/article/john-maxwell-success-or-significance.

lxvii Gass, B., 'Lessons from the Life of David': subsplash.com/ucbcanada/media/mi/+wkxgqgu.

lxviii Twain, M., *The Tragedy of Pudd'nhead Wilson* (ReadHowYouWant, 2008).

lxix Vallotton, K. *Spirit Wars: Winning the Invisible Battle Against Sin and the Enemy*, (Chosen Books, 2012).

lxx Meyer, J., 'Do It Afraid!': joycemeyer.org/everydayanswers/ea-teachings/do-it-afraid.

lxxi Wimber, J., 'Quotes from John Wimber': vineyardusa.org/library/quotes-from-john-wimber.

lxxii Lewis, C.S., cited by Wirt, S.E., 'C. S. Lewis on Heaven, Earth and Outer Space': cbn.com/special/Narnia/articles/ans_LewisLastInterviewB.aspx.

lxxiii Lewis, C.S., *The Last Battle* (Collier Books, 1970).

lxxiv Moody, D.L., cited by Carey, J., '12 of DL Moody's Most Profound Quotes About Faith': relevantmagazine.com/god/12-dl-moodys-most-profound-quotes-about-faith.

lxxv Franklin, J., 'God Owns All the Donuts': youtube.com/watch?v=C3nJJzVYwxY.

lxxvi Goulard, C. and Briggs, D., *Stewardship Impact: Developing a Healthy Stewardship Ministry in the Local Church* (Christian Stewardship Network, 2015).

lxxvii Ten Boom, C. cited by McDaniel, D., '40 Powerful Quotes from Corrie Ten Boom': crosswalk.com/faith/spiritual-life/inspiring-quotes/40-powerful-quotes-from-corrie-ten-boom.html.

lxxviii Jackson Brown H, Jnr., *P.S. I Love You: When Mom Wrote, She Always Saved the Best for Last* (Rutledge Hill Press, 1999).

lxxix Wigglesworth, S. *Ever Increasing Faith* (Whitaker House, 2001).